Paper Matters

TODAY'S PAPER & BOARD INDUSTRY UNFOLDED

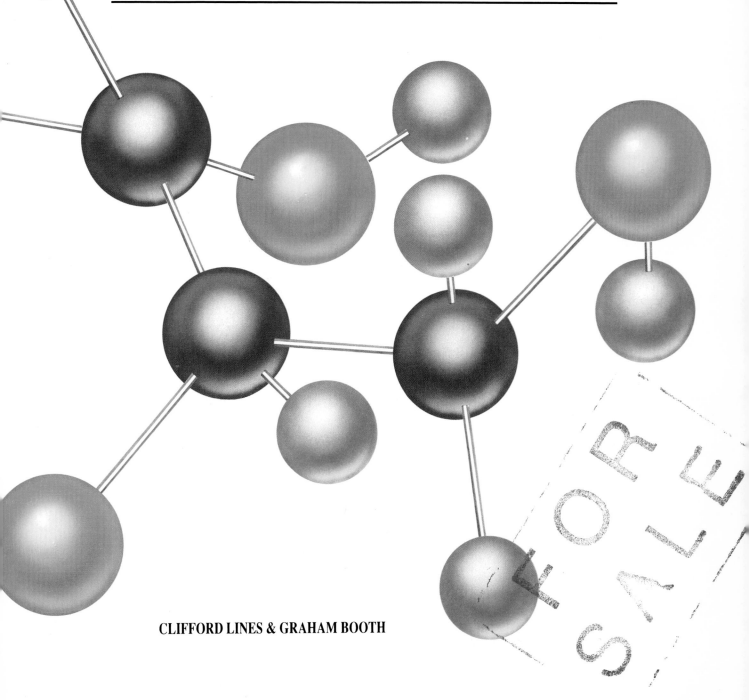

CLIFFORD LINES & GRAHAM BOOTH

First published 1990

Published by Paper Publications Ltd on behalf of the British Paper Industry

Printed and bound by Butler & Tanner Ltd, Frome and London
Text paper 115 g/m^2 Nimrod 2 Smooth from UK Paper Group
Cover board 300 g/m^2 Gemini CIS from G-P Inveresk

A CIP catalogue record for this book is available from the British Library.

ISBN 1 873079 00 1

Acknowledgements
Paper Publications Ltd would like to thank the many people in the paper industry, and beyond, who gave so freely of their time to help with the compilation of this book.
Paper Matters is part of the Paper Industry Resource Pack for schools, which contains wallcharts, teachers' notes, industry directory and a book of paper samples.

The pack is distributed by
The Pulp & Paper Information Centre, Papermakers House, Rivenhall Road, Westlea, Swindon, Wiltshire SN5 7BE,
Telephone (0793) 886086

The Resource Pack items were prepared in 1989 using 1988 statistics. These figures are updated annually and the latest facts and figures are available from the Pulp & Paper Information Centre.

In addition to the companies in the industry who kindly supplied photographs, the publishers and authors wish to thank the following people and organisations for permission to use photographs for which they hold the copyright: Aberdeen Tourist Board: 21I; Heather Angel (Biofotos): 6E (both parts); Bruce Angrave: 26E, 26F; David Bodey: 18B, 18C, 24G; British Coal: 10F; British Gas: 10A; British Printing Industries Federation: 17D, 17E, 17F; J. Allan Cash Ltd: 27B; Bruce Coleman Picture Library: 6G, 6L, 6P, 6U; English China Clays plc: 8B, 8C; Mary Evans Picture Library: 3D, 3I, 5A, 18A; Forestry Commission: 6Q, 6V, 21D, 21E, 21F; Sally and Richard Greenhill Picture Library: 27A; Greenpeace: 21H; Robert Harding Picture Library and the British Museum: 3A, 3B, 3C, 3H; Hulton Deutsch: 6B, 19A; John Mills Photography: 19E; National Portrait Gallery: 3J; Nature Photographers: 6D; Paper Science Dept, UMIST: 4B, 4D; Planet Earth Pictures: 8D; Ann Ronan Picture Library: 1A, 3G, 3L, 11B, 11D; Scottish Tourist Board: 9A; Studio Morgan: 10G, 11A, 18F; The Telegraph Colour Library: 6F, 6R; Threshold Books Ltd: 12A; Times Newspapers Ltd: 6C; Tropix Photographic Library: 20J; Zefa Picture Library (UK) Ltd: 19D

The publishers have made every effort to trace the copyright holders but if they have inadvertently overlooked any, they will be pleased to make the necessary arrangement at the first opportunity.

PAPER

'Over the centuries, no material created by man has made a
greater contribution to civilisation than paper.
Produced from an infinitely renewable source and easily
recycled, its role in communications, protective packaging
and hygiene products is without equal.'

Jeffrey Bartlett, Director General
British Paper & Board Industry Federation

CONTENTS

1 Paper! Paper! Read all about it! — 7
It's a paper world — 7
About this book — 7

2 Living with paper — 9
A wide range of uses — 9
A versatile material — 10
Paper and packaging — 11

3 How it all began — 14
The invention of paper — 14
The first paper mill in Britain — 15
The Industrial Revolution — 16

4 Introduction to papermaking — 19
Preface . . . — 19
What is paper? — 19
The natural raw material of paper — 19
The principle of papermaking — 19
An overview of production — 20

5 Where paper is made — 24
Four main production areas — 24

6 Sources of raw materials: Wood — 27
Forests and the supply of wood pulp — 27
Tree types — 29
Turning wood into pulp — 30
British timber — 34

7 Sources of raw materials: Waste paper — 36
The advantages of recycling paper — 36
Production problems — 37
Fluctuations in demand — 37

8 Sources of raw materials: Additives — 40
Why additives are used — 40
Fillers — 40
Coatings — 41
Sizing paper — 42

9 Sources of raw materials: Water — 44
Water then and water now — 44
Sources of supply — 44
Water used in the production process — 45
Conversion of water to steam — 46

10 Energy — 47
Energy costs — 47

11 Papermaking machines — 50
A fully automated process — 50
Early papermaking machines — 50
Papermaking machines today — 52
Computer control system — 53
Location of the firms — 53

12 The papermaking process — 55
Principles — 55
Stage 1: Stock preparation — 55
Stage 2: Making the sheet
(the wet end) — 56
Stage 3: The dry end — 57

13 The papermakers 1 — 58
Case study: An integrated mill — 58
Britain's newest paper mill — 59
The site — 60
Timber supplies — 60
Other raw materials — 61
Energy — 61
Labour — 61

14 The papermakers 2 — 63
Case study: A non-integrated mill — 63
History of the Dalmore Mill — 63
The mill today — 64

15 The papermakers 3 — 66
Case study: A board mill — 66
A vertically integrated company — 66
Purfleet Board Mills — 67

16 The papermakers 4 — 70
Case study: An international company — 70
Worldwide interests — 70
British locations — 72
Swedish environmental protection — 72

17 Converting — 76
Overview — 76
Printers — 77

18 Packaging — 79
In days gone by . . . — 79
Packaging today — 79
Paper packaging — 81
Board packaging — 81
Corrugated board — 81
The corrugated board manufacturers — 82
Location of manufacturers — 83
The demand for corrugated packaging — 84
Solid board — 84
Cartons — 84
Making cartons — 86

19 Distribution of paper and board — 89
The local market — 89
The evolution of paper and board
merchants — 89
Functions of merchanting — 90
Profile of today's merchants — 92

20	**Overseas trade**	**96**
	Significance of imports	96
	Where imports come from	96
	Types of import	98
	The history of paper imports	98
	Paper agents	101
	Exports	102
	Worldwide consumption of paper and board	103

21	**Paper and the environment**	**106**
	An industry founded on recycling	106
	The supply of fibres: from wood or waste?	106
	Energy	110
	Chemicals	111
	Non-wood fibres	113

22	**Careers in the industry**	**116**
	Papermaking	116
	Career routes in manufacturing	116
	Degrees in paper science	116
	Certificate in paper technology	118
	Sponsored training	118
	Opportunities	118
	Overseas opportunities	119
	People	119
	Careers with paper merchants	119
	Careers in the fibreboard industry	120

23	**Working in the industry**	**122**
	The apprentices	122
	The technical superintendent	123
	The product manager	124
	The sales office manager	125

24	**The future**	**126**
	Opportunities	126
	Research	126
	Investment in the future	128
	The challenge of the 1990s	130

25	**Experiments with paper**	**131**
	1 Testing the direction of the fibres	131
	2 Checking paper for expansion due to moisture	132
	3 Checking for water absorption	133
	4 Fibre identification tests	133
	5 Testing paper strength	134
	6 Making recycled paper	134
	7 Grammage test	135

26	**Creative work with paper**	**136**
	Introduction	136
	Cutting shapes	136
	Paper engineering	136
	Origami	137
	Papier maché	137
	Designs with artstraws	138
	Paper sculpture	138
	Collage and mosaic	139

| 27 | **Ideas for school coursework** | **140** |
| | How to organise coursework | 140 |

28	**Glossary**	**143**
29	**Answers to questions**	**146**
30	**Index**	**150**

Foreword

The introduction of the National Curriculum and the importance attached to economic and industrial understanding, coupled with the national impetus to develop education and business partnerships, makes the last decade of this millenium a watershed in the development of our society. These overarching ingredients of the macro environment create an enormous opportunity for educationalists and industrialists to cooperate for the benefit of the whole community, not just in the next decade but into the next century.

These resources, created by the paper industry, are an enormous help to teachers and to members of schools' local economic communities to enable them to work together to develop students' understanding of business, the economy and the paper industry. By utilising these excellent materials and by working together to bring industry to life in schools and bring relevant contexts to the learning of students, both the imperatives of personal and economic growth can be achieved simultaneously.

Jack Peffers
National Coordinator SCIP

SCHOOL CURRICULUM INDUSTRY PARTNERSHIP

IT'S A PAPER WORLD

Paper is a remarkable product. Can you think of any other manufactured item which frequently finishes up measuring 210 mm × 297 mm and can be bought for less than 0.5 of a penny, that requires an investment of at least £50 million to produce, and can be made at over 60 mph?

Many billions of sheets of wafer-thin paper are made, yet the finished product is extremely uniform and is produced to the highest standards of technical excellence. Paper is also environmentally friendly as the natural cellulose fibres of which it is made can be used again and again. Eventually it is **biodegradable** and will decompose naturally without causing pollution.

Paper was first made in Britain about 500 years ago. This makes it one of the country's oldest industries. From its humble beginnings the paper industry has grown into a mature and stable sector of the economy. It employs thousands of people and the demand for its products is continually increasing.

In the UK today, we each use an average of about 163 kg of paper a year. Some people say that paper is becoming less important in the modern world but this is incorrect. Although offices are computerised and plastic is often substituted for paper in bags and wrapping material, new uses are constantly being found for paper and board. The introduction of computers has increased rather than decreased demand.

B Paper is now produced at 60 mph on reels weighing up to 20 tonnes

ABOUT THIS BOOK

This book sets out to explain the structure and working of this fascinating industry whose products we all use in many ways every day of the year. You will see it is similar to many of your school books. It provides information and also includes a variety of activities so that you can find out about the industry for yourself. It also contains ideas which will help you to design coursework projects on paper or the papermaking industry.

This book is about paper, one of the essentials of modern life, and about the people who produce it. Carrying out the activities will help to reinforce your knowledge and understanding. You will also gain valuable experience in a range of skills, such as calculating and classifying, which are important elements of many of the subjects you are studying.

A A water-powered paper mill in the 1600s

1C The paper industry employs thousands of people

Finally, you will have a greater appreciation of the career opportunities which exist in the paper industry. The industry needs people who are interested in high tech developments and who are keen to follow a career in the paper trade. It is an industry that provides extensive training schemes, university scholarships and excellent promotion prospects.

THINGS TO DO

To start you off on the activities make a bar chart of the following statistics.

TABLE 1.1

UK Production of paper and board (thousand tonnes)	
1981	3380
1982	3198
1983	3298
1984	3591
1985	3681
1986	3941
1987	4183
1988	4295
1989	4476

A WIDE RANGE OF USES

Because we are familiar with two or three types of **paper**, such as writing paper, newsprint and toilet paper, we fail to appreciate the enormous range that is available. Each type of paper or **board** (the trade's name for cardboard) is designed for a particular purpose. For example, the paper used in this book has been specially treated so that it can be printed on and can carry clear and accurate reproductions of colour photographs. By contrast, paper handkerchiefs are made of soft, thin paper which is absorbent. Newspapers are printed on cheap paper to keep costs down because they have a short life, whereas many magazines use more expensive, higher quality paper.

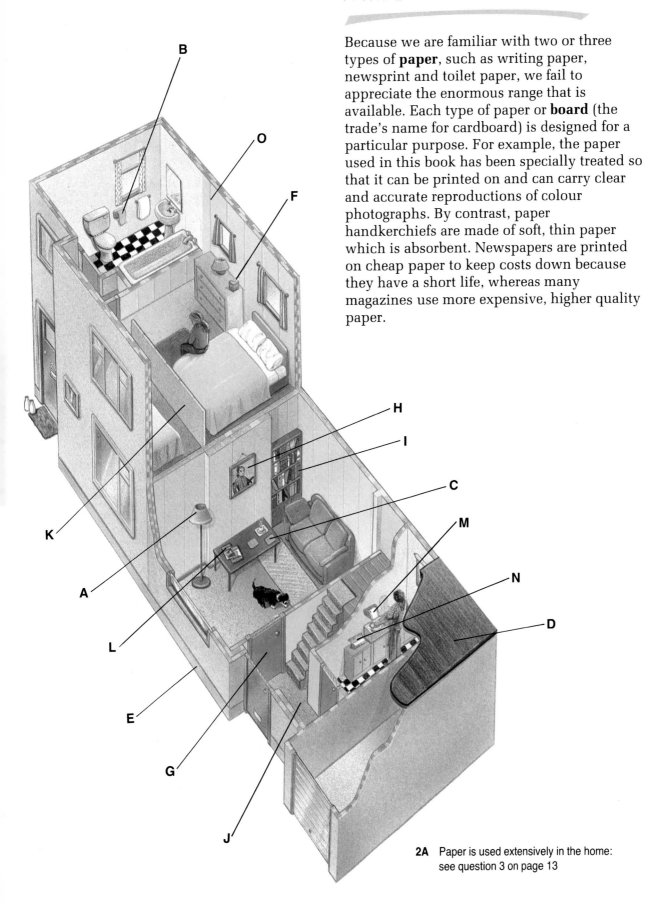

2A Paper is used extensively in the home: see question 3 on page 13

A VERSATILE MATERIAL

We depend on paper throughout our lives and its range of uses seems limitless. It is extremely versatile and can be waterproofed, waxed, coated, glazed, printed, moulded, laminated and crêped. Some of its uses seem to contradict one another. It can be made to burn (e.g. cigarette paper) or made fire-resistant (e.g. Christmas decorations). It can be tough enough to use in a car engine, or soft enough for a baby's napkin. It can be made opaque, translucent or transparent, water absorbent or moistureproof. It can be laminated with itself or laminated to fabric, plastics or metal. It can be recycled many times to save both energy and timber resources. Some types of paper, such as newsprint, are cheap and made in large quantities, while handmade paper is very expensive and is only produced in very small amounts.

Later in this book we shall look at some of the processes that give paper these distinctive qualities and at the raw materials such as water and wood from which paper is made.

2B How many different uses of paper can you see?

10

3D Early papermaking in China, using plant fibres

THE FIRST PAPER MILL IN BRITAIN

We are not certain of the exact year when paper was first made in Britain, but it was probably in the 1480s because the first mill was well-established by 1494. The site was a watermill on the River Beane just outside Hertford. It was owned by John Tate, a merchant who had travelled on the Continent where he must have seen paper being made. There is a mill on the same spot today but it no longer makes paper. Water from the river was used to wash and soften the rags which were then beaten into a pulp. Only white rags could be used because chemical bleaches were unknown. The river also provided the power needed to drive a waterwheel. This

wheel worked heavy wooden hammers called **stampers**. These pulped the rags and separated the fibres.

Skilled men made the paper by hand using the Chinese method. The sheets, which must have looked something like blotting paper, were hung up to dry and then coated with animal glue. This had the effect of **sizing** the paper so that it could be used for writing and printing.

We can identify Tate's paper by a **watermark** which he used. This was in the form of a star inside a double circle. The design was pressed into the wet paper with wires so that the paper was slightly thinner and

3F

allowed more light through. Later a Tudor rose was used, probably in honour of visits to Hertford by King Henry VII in 1498 and 1499. The King's Household Accounts Book contains the entry *'for a rewarde geven at the paper mylne 16s 8d'*. The following year a reward of 6s 8d was given. No doubt the King received gifts of paper which prompted the rewards.

John Tate died in 1507 and his mill was sold and was not used again for making paper. There is no evidence of another paper mill in Britain until 1554 when one began operating near Cambridge, making brown wrapping paper. White paper was imported from Europe and it was not made again in Britain

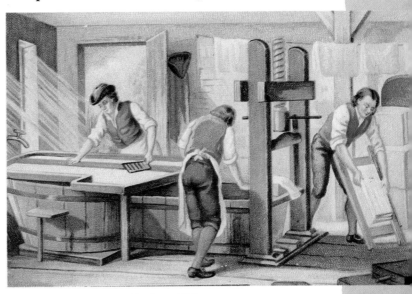

3E The location of John Tate's mill at Hertford

3G Making paper by hand in about 1700

15

until 1588 when a mill was started at Dartford in Kent.

A number of small mills were set up in Hertfordshire in the 17th and 18th centuries. Their location shows that papermaking was a rural industry, which needed to be near water for power and for the basic processes. The mills were also near enough to London to obtain rags from the city and surrounding towns. Throughout Europe rags were the principal source of cellulose fibre for papermaking until the mid-1800s. Paper was made by hand for local markets and there was little transportation of either raw materials or the manufactured paper.

THE INDUSTRIAL REVOLUTION

After about 1750 papermaking, like other industries, went through a period of fairly rapid improvement and change. New machinery was invented and steam was used instead of water power to drive the machines.

The quality of paper was improved in the 1740s by James Whatman and his son at Turkey Mill near Maidstone in Kent. They produced a smooth writing paper, known as **wove paper**, and special papers which could be used for printing pictures, maps and navigational charts. In 1792 chlorine was introduced as a bleach to whiten the rags used by the industry. The first paper produced was, however, liable to fall apart after a short time because the bleach was too strong.

3I Women were employed to cut and sort old cotton rags

One of the most important dates connected with the industry is 1803. This was when the first mechanical papermaking machine in the world was introduced. The machine was invented in France by Nicholas Robert and installed at Frogmore Mill in Hertfordshire.

3J Henry Fourdrinier (on the right) and Bryan Donkin

3H Paper maps and navigational charts were used from the early 17th century

The mill was owned by two wealthy London stationers, Henry and Sealy **Fourdrinier**, who gave their name to the machine. They spent a lot of money and employed an engineer called Bryan Donkin to improve the design. It used a moving belt made of a wire mesh as a base for the wet pulp. The water drained through the mesh leaving the fibre behind as a sheet which was then cut into sections and hung up to dry.

Another machine was developed in 1809 by John Dickinson at a nearby mill. He used a rotating cylinder covered with wire mesh to collect the fibres and form a sheet of paper. This was carried along a moving belt to be pressed between rollers to remove some of the water. Later steam-heated cylinders were added to dry the paper more quickly.

In 1825 John and Christopher Phipps, who had mills at Dover, invented a **dandy roll** which helped to press out some of the water on the Fourdrinier machine. By including wire designs on this roll, watermarks could be added to the paper. This idea was developed by William Joynson of St Mary Cray, Kent, in 1839. He patented the idea of adding letters or other shapes to the surface of the dandy roll so that they pressed further into the wet pulp and left **watermarks**. Further engineering improvements during the 19th century and the use of steam power helped speed up the papermaking operation dramatically at a time when the demand for paper was increasing rapidly.

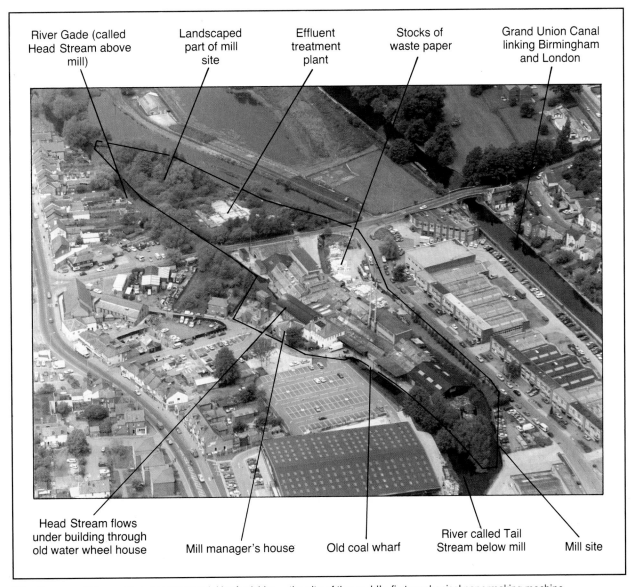

River Gade (called Head Stream above mill)

Landscaped part of mill site

Effluent treatment plant

Stocks of waste paper

Grand Union Canal linking Birmingham and London

Head Stream flows under building through old water wheel house

Mill manager's house

Old coal wharf

River called Tail Stream below mill

Mill site

3K Frogmore Mill near Hemel Hempstead, Hertfordshire – the site of the world's first mechanical papermaking machine

A shortage of rags held back the growth of the industry and other fibres had to be introduced. The shortage was solved by the use of wood pulp. In 1857 a process was invented in Germany in which wood was ground up to separate the fibres. An alternative method was invented in Britain by Watt and Burgess in 1864. In this method the wood was pressure-cooked with chemicals which dissolved out **lignin**, the chemical which sticks the individual fibres together. As a result of these inventions the demand for wood pulp increased rapidly in the second half of the 19th century.

In Britain there were no large supplies of wood available. Consequently, paper mills developed on rivers near to ports where there was not only a suitable source of water for the manufacturing process, but where imported supplies of wood pulp could be brought close to the mill. The development of new machinery and the increasing demand for paper meant that countries rich in forest resources, such as Germany, Austria, Czechoslovakia and Scandinavia, became important pulp and paper areas.

Canada and the USA also had large forest resources and paper industries developed there too. During World War II the UK had to rely on North America for supplies of pulp and paper. British mills used straw as a raw material. The recycling of waste paper also became more important.

THINGS TO DO

1 Make a time chart showing important dates and events in the history of papermaking in Britain. Start with:

| 1488 | possible date when John Tate started making paper at Hertford |

2 Look at the map 3E, showing the site of Tate's Mill and the aerial photograph 3K of the Frogmore Mill.
   (a) Why were both mills located on rivers?
   (b) Why were they built fairly close to the centres of population?
   (c) Why was the Frogmore Mill in a good position when steam power was introduced to drive the machinery?
   (d) Why does the water passing through a waterwheel need to be controlled by building sluices and weirs upstream, and providing an overspill channel?

3 What other industries developed near watermills before steam power was introduced? How was the water power used by these industries?

4 Imagine your family owned a papermaking mill. Design a family watermark for paper made at the mill.

5 Look at photo 3G and explain the following features.
   (a) the function of the screw press
   (b) what the large vat is used for
   (c) what else would have to be done to the sheets of paper hanging up to dry before they could be used for printing or writing.

3L The Industrial Revolution brought mechanisation

PREFACE . . .

This chapter will give you an introduction to the process of making paper and to the raw materials used.

The following chapters give much more information about the raw materials, where they come from and how they are used by the papermaker. Where paper is made and the equipment used in its manufacture is also explained. Chapter 12 deals with the complete process of papermaking and then in chapters 13, 14, 15 and 16 some case studies show how the principle has been adapted by three very different types of mill.

To help you learn as much as possible from these chapters, it is worthwhile outlining the principle of papermaking first.

WHAT IS PAPER?

In simple terms paper can be described as a web-like material made of vegetable fibres and usually blended or coated with various chemicals to produce a required texture and finish.

The vegetable fibre is cellulose which is extracted from wood. Both **coniferous** and **deciduous** or **broadleaved** trees are used. Other plant fibres such as cotton, flax, hemp, bamboo, sugar cane and cereal straw can also be sources of cellulose, but today wood is the most widely used source for papermaking.

THE NATURAL RAW MATERIAL OF PAPER

The cell walls of all green land plants are largely made of the complex carbohydrate **cellulose**, $(C_6H_{10}O_5)n$, which is synthesised by the cells. Cellulose belongs to a group of natural carbohydrates called **polysaccharides** which are built up by the combination of many molecules of **monosaccharides,** or simple sugars.

As each box-shaped cell grows, cellulose is deposited on the walls which thicken and become hard. At the same time a number of other substances, mainly lignin, are also produced by the cell. These are fused into the cell wall and make it strong and rigid. Lignification of the cell wall is followed by the death of the liquid **protoplasm**, or living part, of the cell. This leaves a hollow tube of cellulose bound together with the **glutinous** (sticky) lignin. A string of similar dead cells group together into **fibrils** which in turn combine to form the fibre.

Wood is composed largely of lignified cells and lignin can account for up to 25% of the wood. Cellulose is hard, colourless, readily absorbs water but is insoluble in water. Much of the plant material we eat consists of it. It cannot be digested and is the well-known **fibre roughage** in our diet.

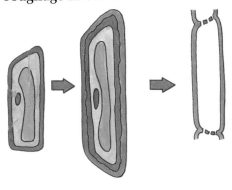

4A How cells in wood grow and become lignified

THE PRINCIPLE OF PAPERMAKING

The method developed in China nearly 2000 years ago is still the basis of making paper and board today. The principle used is that cellulose fibres naturally link together under certain conditions.

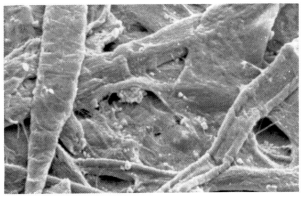

4B Electron micrograph of paper surface magnified 640 times

When a suspension of the fibres in water is poured over a fine sieve the water drains away. As it does so the fibres sink down to the surface of the sieve. When the fibres touch, they lock together. This produces a complete but fragile **web**. When more water is removed the bonding becomes stronger. This happens as the web of paper passes through the paper machine, getting drier all the time. Ironically, water is needed to form the chemical bond between the fibres and this is why paper contains about 6% water.

Cellulose fibres from different plants are not all the same and these differences, together with the treatment processes they go through at the pulping stage, are used by papermakers to produce various grades and strengths of paper.

Board is heavier, thicker and more rigid than paper and is made from several layers of pulp. Very thick board is made by sticking together sheets of paper or board. This process is called **laminating.**

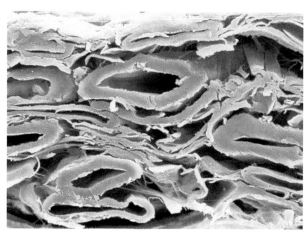

4D Electron micrograph of cross-section of *The Guardian* magnified 750 times

AN OVERVIEW OF PRODUCTION

Nearly all the paper mills in Britain buy wood pulp or waste paper as their raw material. Most wood pulp is made in overseas pulp mills and shipped to Britain in bales.

There are only five mills in the UK which start with wood and finish with paper. The trees – cut down as **thinnings** – are cut into logs and ground into **mechanical pulp** which is used to make the paper. The combined pulp and paper mills are amongst the largest and are called **integrated** mills.

Diagram 4E shows how the manufacture of paper can be described as a **system** or pattern of inputs, processes and outputs which are linked to one another. It illustrates how the system operates throughout the industry as a whole. A systems diagram for an individual mill will differ in some respects from this generalised model.

Paper production uses large amounts of water – up to 40 000 litres are needed to make one tonne of paper or board. Only a small amount is **consumed** in the production processes. Most of the water is recycled many times and any returned to the rivers or lakes is thoroughly cleaned and treated before it enters the drainage system.

Energy is a key component of the efficiency equation in manufacturing. Mills use coal, oil, gas and electricity as energy sources and significant improvements in energy use have been made during the last eight years (see Chapter 10).

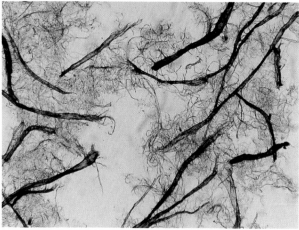

4C Stained cotton fibres before (top) and after refining (bottom)

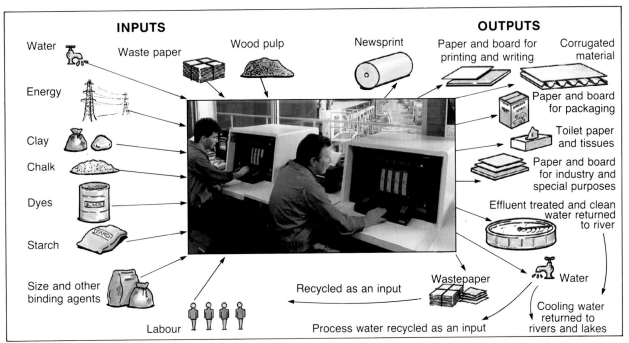

INPUTS

Water
Waste paper
Wood pulp
Energy
Clay
Chalk
Dyes
Starch
Size and other binding agents
Labour

OUTPUTS

Newsprint
Paper and board for printing and writing
Corrugated material
Paper and board for packaging
Toilet paper and tissues
Paper and board for industry and special purposes
Effluent treated and clean water returned to river
Water
Cooling water returned to rivers and lakes

Recycled as an input
Wastepaper
Process water recycled as an input

4E Inputs and outputs of the paper and board industry

Paper's great versatility is the result of the ability of cellulose to combine with many types of chemical additives. This enables papers with a wide range of specifications to be produced. In addition, some papers are also coated with a mixture of chemicals to achieve certain characteristics. Chapter 8 explains about additives in papermaking.

The final input to the system is the **workforce**, without which the system would not exist. Increasing automation, the use of computers and the introduction of new machinery has created a demand for skilled workers. About 33 000 people are employed by the mills and three-quarters of any mill's workforce is likely to be concerned with manufacturing processes or maintenance. The other quarter consists of managers, sales personnel, technicians, supervisors, administrators, office staff and researchers.

4F Papermaking involves administrative staff as well as machine technicians and research scientists

21

Table 4.1 shows the types of paper and board which form the industry's output. These are grouped under six headings.

TABLE 4.1 Production 1988

Category		Thousand tonnes	% of total
Newsprint		529	12.3
Paper for printing and writing		1216	28.3
Corrugated case material		1127	26.2
Packaging papers and board		694	16.2
Hygiene papers		439	10.2
Industrial and special purpose paper and board		290	6.8
Total		4295	100

Paperfax

- It took nearly 1400 years for the art of papermaking to travel from China to England.
- A watermark is made by pressing a roll carrying a pattern, called a **dandy roll**, into wet pulp.
- A modern papermaking machine is as long as a football pitch.
- One of the most valuable pieces of paper in the world is a German stamp which was sold in 1985 for £615 000.

FORESTS AND THE SUPPLY OF WOOD PULP

Wood is the paper industry's primary raw material. It was not always so. Until about 130 years ago old rags were the main raw material because no one knew how to make wood pulp.

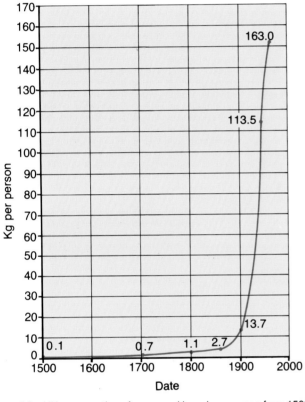

6A UK consumption of paper and board per person from 1500

The demand for rags exceeded the supply as the industry grew rapidly after the Industrial Revolution. The surging demand for paper was caused by its increased use in society. And society itself was expanding and becoming urbanised. In 1801 the UK's population was 16 million but this almost doubled to 29 million by 1861. In addition, more people were being educated so more books were needed. Faster printing techniques rapidly used up supplies of paper and communication was improving with the introduction of more newspapers.

Add to this the improvements in paper manufacturing and it is easy to see that supplies of secondhand cotton rags were

6B Books were used in education many years ago

6C *The Times* – a first edition!

6D Esparto grass which can be used as a source of fibre in papermaking

insufficient to feed this growing industry. From about 1830 the search was on for an alternative source of fibres to rags. The need was partly met by increasing the import of rags from Europe and by using **esparto grass** from North Africa and Spain. In addition, used paper was starting to be recycled.

For many years scientists had known that wasps chewed tree bark and made from it a fibrous tissue to build their nests. But it was not until 1857 that a suitable process was developed to grind wood to separate out the fibres. From then on wood progressed to become the industry's main source of 'new' fibre.

In many parts of the world, including Britain, trees are a crop to be farmed and harvested in a similar way to wheat or potatoes, although with a longer time span. Fortunately trees can often be grown where other crops would fail. To give the industry an environmentally secure future and to guarantee future supplies, new trees are planted to replace those that have reached maturity and are felled. Turn to Chapter 21, Paper and the Environment, for more information about trees.

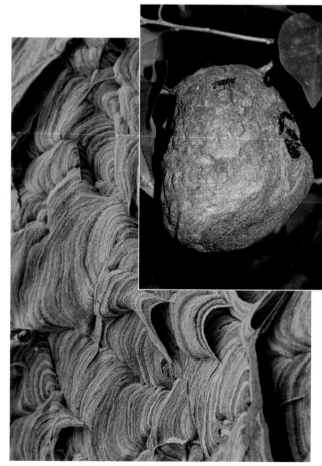

6E The surface of the nest of the common wasp; it is like paper Inset is a photo of a wasp's nest from Guyana

TREE TYPES

6F Pine and spruce are widely used as sources of fibre

Almost any tree can be used to make pulp but some species give fibres that are particularly suitable for papermaking. Each type of tree produces cellulose fibres with unique characteristics which give paper made from that type of wood special properties. The different speeds at which trees grow produce variations in the fibres. For example, a pine tree grown in the northern part of Finland, where growth is very slow, produces thinner fibres than one grown in the warmer southern region of the country. The way the pulp is made also helps to determine the qualities of the paper. Very dense species of tropical hardwoods are not used for papermaking.

6G Northern pines – they may take 70 years to grow this size

6H Fast-growing eucalyptus trees, originally from Australia

The first species of tree to be used in great quantities were pine and spruce from the cool northern climates of Europe and North America. They are still preferred for many uses but in addition, birch and eucalyptus have become popular. Eucalyptus is a fast-growing tree that thrives in many countries including Spain, Portugal, Brazil and its native Australia. It takes only seven to ten years before it is ready for converting into pulp, compared with up to 70 years for the very northern conifers. The southern pines from the USA and parts of Central and South America, Africa and Asia are also becoming more important. In Britain wood comes from Forestry Commission land or private estates in the highland regions of the west and north. Spruce and pine are the main types but birch and beech are also used.

Crops of conifers used to make softwood pulp are thinned about 20-25 years after planting. These thinnings are used for making wood pulp and as a source of energy. More trees are being planted to meet the rising demand for wood pulp. Planting is done imaginatively and much marginal land is being made productive.

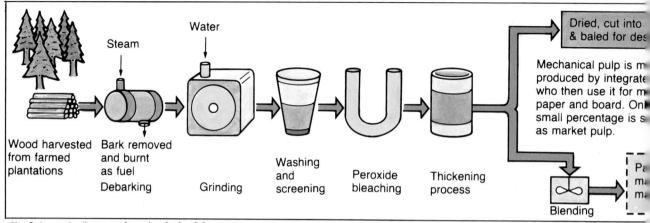

Steam

Water

Dried, cut into
& baled for des

Mechanical pulp is m
produced by integrate
who then use it for m
paper and board. On
small percentage is s
as market pulp.

Wood harvested from farmed plantations

Bark removed and burnt as fuel
Debarking

Grinding

Washing and screening

Peroxide bleaching

Thickening process

Blending

P
ma
ma

6I Schematic diagram of mechanical pulping

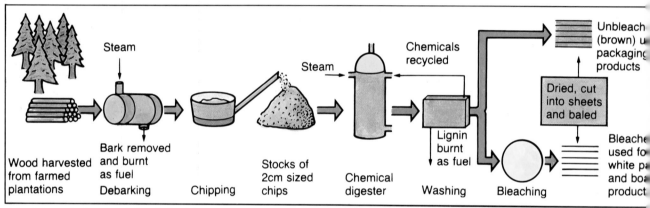

Steam

Steam

Chemicals recycled

Unbleach
(brown) u
packaging
products

Dried, cut
into sheets
and baled

Lignin burnt as fuel

Bleache
used fo
white pa
and boa
product

Wood harvested from farmed plantations

Bark removed and burnt as fuel
Debarking

Chipping

Stocks of 2cm sized chips

Chemical digester

Washing

Bleaching

6J Schematic diagram of chemical pulping

The two processes used for turning wood into pulp produce **chemical pulp** and **mechanical pulp**. Mechanical pulp which yields over 90% of the wood as fibre is produced by forcing debarked logs, about two metres long, and hot water between enormous rotating steel discs with teeth which literally tear the wood apart. Alternatively, whole logs can be pressed against grindstones which is why this type of is also known as **groundwood** pulp.

6K   Tree felling

6L   Harvesting trees with a tractor

6M   Digester towers used in chemical pulping

6O   Logs are debarked in the orange cylinder

Virtually the whole of the debarked log is turned into pulp. This means it contains lignin, the binding material which holds the cellulose fibres together. Lignin is sensitive to light and turns brown, which explains why papers made from mechanical pulp will discolour. Consequently, mechanical pulp is used when it does not matter if, in time, the paper loses its whiteness, as happens with newspapers. The special advantages of

mechanical pulp are that it makes the paper opaque and bulky. It is also less expensive than chemical pulp which has a ratio of finished fibre to raw wood input of about 50%, the remainder providing a renewable source of energy for the process.

To produce chemical pulp, the smaller diameter wood, which makes up about 45% of the original tree and is too small for sawn timber, is cut into 2 cm chips. These are then pressure-cooked in a large **digester** to which chemicals have been added, to separate the lignin from the cellulose fibres. The lignin and chemicals are washed out of the pulp and recovered for further use. The lignin is burnt and provides enough energy to run a modern pulp mill. The process is **self-sufficient** in terms of energy. This means that it produces

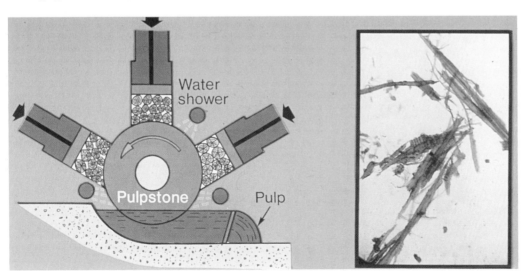

6N
The groundwood pulping process. This produces bundles of fibres which may be damaged

31

6P Rafts of logs are floated down to the pulp mills

as much energy as it uses. The cellulose fibres form a brown pulp which can be used for making packaging products such as corrugated cases. Some of the pulp is bleached and used for white paper and board. The chemical pulp process produces fibres that are stronger than those produced by grinding. However, chemical pulp can only be produced profitably in a large plant using expensive machinery. If not properly managed the chemicals used could damage the environment, so careful design and proper equipment must be used to prevent pollution. Strangely, paper made from pulp produced by this method is called **wood-free.** What this really means is wood-based paper free from mechanical pulp which contains impurities such as lignin.

Limited quantities of pulp are produced by processes which first soften the fibre chemically and then pull it apart mechanically. These are known by a variety of names such as **chemi-thermo mechanical** pulp, **semi-chemical** pulp, etc. They are a compromise between the mechanical and chemical processes.

6Q Successive thinnings of conifer plantations open up the crop and encourage ground vegetation

The freshly produced pulp in slush form can be converted immediately into paper or, alternatively, it can be dried, made into sheets, baled and sold to non-integrated mills. In 1988 Britain imported 1.69 million tonnes of wood pulp. The vast majority of this was chemical pulp used to make top quality paper. These imports account for 40% of the fibre raw material used by British paper mills. Sales of imported wood pulp are handled by companies who are usually members of the **British Wood Pulp Association.**

Although the UK paper and board industry has considerably increased its output during the 1980s, the import of wood pulp has only increased slightly. This is partly because more waste paper is being used and partly because new integrated mills are using British timber resources. Of the 2.1 million tonnes of wood pulp used in British paper mills in 1988, 80% was imported, mainly from Canada, Sweden, Finland, the USA, Portugal and Spain.

6S Bales of dried pulp being unloaded at the docks

6T The British Wood Pulp Association logo

6R Helicopter logging in British Columbia

6U A Norwegian pulp mill on the River Tinnelva

33

6V The Forestry Commission's Kielder Forest, which won an award for wildlife conservation

BRITISH TIMBER

British wood goes to five large integrated mills at Newport in Gwent, Shotton in Clywd, Sittingbourne in Kent, Workington in Cumbria and Irvine in Strathclyde. These mills are likely to expand their production of newsprint, carton board and coated paper for magazines, travel brochures and catalogues. They already export some of their paper to Europe, the Middle East and North America.

These five paper mills take a variety of home-grown timber. Iggesund Paperboard in Cumbria, Caledonian Paper at Irvine and Shotton Paper depend mainly on sitka spruce to which is added some fir and hemlock. St Regis Paper at Newport and in Kent use mainly waste wood from various sources which, after pulping, is blended with recycled paper and board. These mills operate for 24 hours a day, nearly every day of the year, and require very large quantities of clean, high-quality timber.

Timber supplies will increase in the 1990s as Forestry Commission land planted 20 or more years ago produces coniferous trees of a suitable size for the mills. After the year 2000 more private forests will be ready for felling to meet the expected increase in demand.

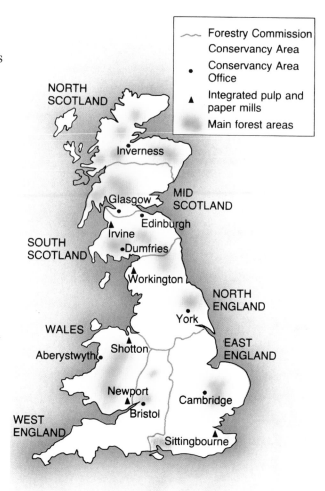

Forestry Commission Conservancy Area

• Conservancy Area Office

▲ Integrated pulp and paper mills

Main forest areas

NORTH SCOTLAND

Inverness

Glasgow

MID SCOTLAND

Edinburgh

Irvine

SOUTH SCOTLAND

•Dumfries

Workington

NORTH ENGLAND

York

WALES

EAST ENGLAND

Aberystwyth•

Shotton

Newport

Cambridge

WEST ENGLAND

Bristol

Sittingbourne

6W Integrated pulp and paper mills and forests in the UK

THINGS TO DO

1 Make a copy of diagram 7H below and write in the correct places the following information. The information is not listed in the correct order.
transport to mill
waste paper merchants — cleaning, sorting and baling
mill — cleaning, removing contraries from pulp
offices
private homes
factories
supermarkets
transport to waste paper merchants
sources of waste paper

2 Make a survey of the types and amounts of waste paper which build up in your home over a period of *one week*. Weigh the quantities each day and make a chart like Table 7.1 to record the results of your survey.

3 What happens to waste paper in your district? Is it collected separately from other rubbish? Find out where it goes after it has been collected. Draw a diagram with sketches as a summary of what you have found out.

4 You have been given *three minutes* by your local radio station to make an appeal for people to collect waste paper for recycling. Write down what you would say. Read it aloud to your friends and ask them for their comments.

5 Design a poster encouraging people to take their old newspapers to a central collection point in your area.

TABLE 7.1

Day	Cardboard (weight)	Newspaper (weight)	Other waste paper (weight)	Total (weight)
Sunday				
Monday				
Tuesday				
Wednesday				
Thursday				
Friday				
Saturday				
Grand totals				

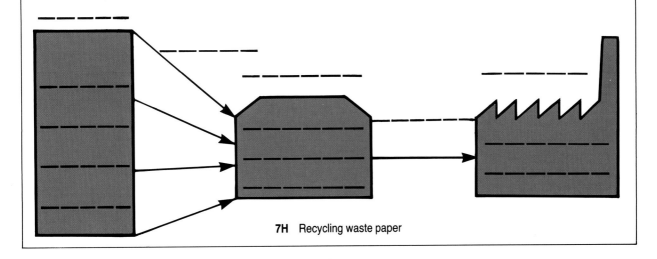

7H Recycling waste paper

WHY ADDITIVES ARE USED

The paper we use is not just a mesh of fibres. It also contains other raw materials which have been added to give it certain properties such as whiteness or strength. These other raw materials are called **additives**. They are supplied to the papermakers by a number of specialist companies in Britain and overseas. Between 5% and 35% of the weight of one tonne of paper is made up of these additives in the form of **minerals**, **chemicals** and **dyes**. Each grade of paper and board requires a very accurate blend of pulps and additives and the properties of the paper are continually monitored by computers during manufacture.

Additives are applied in two different ways. They can be used as **fillers** or **loadings** which are blended with the watery pulp suspension known as the **stock**. The stock is the mixture pumped onto the papermaking machine.

Additives can also be used as **coatings** which are put onto the paper to give it specific properties.

Some additives are used as both fillers and coatings.

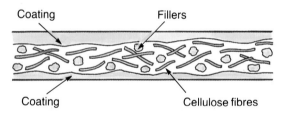

8A Section through paper showing fillers and coatings

FILLERS

The main purpose of fillers is literally to fill the spaces between the mesh of interlinked cellulose fibres, so that a solid, smooth and level surface is achieved. This is important if the paper is going to be used for writing or printing. As well as changing the latticework of fibres into a compact sheet, fillers improve the **opacity** (the non-transparent quality) of the paper by packing the gaps between the fibres. Fillers are sometimes used as a substitute for fibres because they are cheaper than fibre but too much filler makes the paper weak.

8B Open-cast quarries in Cornwall, extracting china clay

8C Extraction of china clay using high-pressure water jets

China clay (hydrated aluminium silicate, $Al_2 2SiO_2.2H_2O$) is by far the most common filler as it is cheap and of high quality. China clay is also known as **kaolin** called after the Kuling (Kaoling) mountain range in China where it was first mined. In Britain china clay comes from the English China Clay Company's open cast quarries near St Austell in Cornwall. The clay is worked, treated to remove impurities, sieved and dried to a fine powder. The same clay is used by other British industries for porcelain, in paint making and in cosmetics.

Titanium dioxide (TiO_2) is a naturally occurring metallic compound found in practically all igneous rocks. The oxide is used as a high-grade white pigment. It is an expensive additive and is mainly used to give added whiteness and opacity to very thin papers that need to retain their strength, e.g. airmail paper.

Chalk (calcium carbonate, $CaCO_3$) is a soft, fine-grained whitish rock compound widely available in Europe. In Britain the English China Clay Company provides the paper industry with chalk from its quarries in Wiltshire and Yorkshire. Chalk is a cheap filler and, like china clay, improves the opacity of paper. In the past there was some difficulty in using chalk because it reacted with other acidic chemicals used in papermaking. Today this problem has been largely solved and chalk has become a useful and cheap additive.

Talc (hydrated magnesium silicate, $3Mg0.4SiO_2.H_2O$) is a minor filler which gives the paper a smoothness and softness.

Other important additives that are blended into the stock before it goes onto the papermaking machine are pigments and dyes which act as colouring agents.

Pigments are inorganic mineral substances that colour the paper by filling the spaces between the fibres in the same way as loadings. Unlike dyes, they do not penetrate the fibres themselves. Prussian blue (potassium ferric ferrocyanide) is an example of a well-known pigment.

Dyes are chemical substances which can penetrate or **fix** themselves to the cellulose fibres and are **fast** to light and water. Dyes used to be extracted from plants but modern dyes are all made artificially, often from coal-tar by-products. Many are related to the complex organic compound **aniline**, and are known as **aniline dyes**. A very wide range of coloured dyes is available and they can be mixed to produce numerous shades.

8D Extraction of chalk

8E Dyes and pigments used in papermaking

COATINGS

Even after fillers have been added to the fibrous mesh, seen through the microscope the surface of the paper looks like a series of hills and valleys. These can be flattened out to some degree by running the paper through a series of rollers, but the only way to give the paper a completely smooth and flat surface is by coating it. The coating fills in the valleys in the same way as Polyfilla can be used by a decorator to smooth out the surface irregularities of a wall he is about to paint.

It is most important that paper which is going to be used for printing and writing has a smooth surface. This allows the printer to reproduce text and illustrations in sharp detail with very little variation in colour. For instance the pages of this book are made from a coated paper, in this case with a **matt** finish.

The most common coating applied to paper is made from especially fine china clay, often mixed with some titanium dioxide. The clay gives the paper smoothness and gloss and the titanium dioxide improves the whiteness. The coating makes the paper feel thin as well as shiny. Coated papers are used for high quality magazines and china clay can account for up to one-third of the weight of these magazines.

8F Inclusion of additives is carefully monitored

Adhesive substances called **binders** are also part of the surface coating mixture. These stick the coating to the exposed surface fibres of the paper. **Casein** (a protein of milk), **latex** and **starch** are examples of natural binders. Synthetic binders are also used.

Some coatings are applied to the paper towards the end of the manufacturing process but most coatings are put on in a separate process after the paper has been made.

SIZING PAPER

Another very important process is the addition of sizing agents to some papers. Sizing prevents any water-based inks from spreading out, or **feathering**, as they do on blotting paper which is not sized. Sizing also adds to the surface strength and stiffness of the paper. For printing and writing papers these factors are critical. In some packaging

8G The size press where a coating of starch is added

papers size is also applied to help limit the **water up-take** (the amount of water absorbed) during the manufacturing process or in the product's final use. Some grades of paper are virtually waterproof.

Sizing could be described as putting a transparent, moisture-resistant glaze on paper. In the early days of papermaking this was achieved by dipping handmade paper into a tub of **gelatine** and then squeezing it between rollers like a mangle.

This same principle is applied today, but the process has been brought up to date technically and is part of the fully automated papermaking process. Gelatine is still sometimes used as a sizing substance.

8H The web of paper passes through the size press

Sizing can be carried out in two ways. The process is called **internal sizing** when the anti-water absorption agents are added to the stock before the paper is made. This method of sizing, sometimes also called **engine sizing**, is important to stop the spread of water-based writing inks but will not prevent the penetration of oil-based printing inks. This has to be dealt with at a later stage in the manufacturing process.

Rosin which is made from the resin of pine trees has been used as the principal ingredient for internal sizing. It also helps to stick the fibres together. The disadvantage of rosin is that it also requires another additive, **alum**, for its successful application. Alum leaves acidic residues in the paper which make it deteriorate over time. Today more than half the sized papers produced in the UK use neutral synthetic sizes rather than the traditional rosin and alum solutions.

Sizing is also applied as a specialised coating halfway through the manufacturing process — at the **size press**. Here a starch-based solution is pressed on to the surface of the moving paper by the size press rolls. The starch acts as an adhesive to bind the surface together and this helps prevent **fibre lift** during printing. This coating resists the penetration of the oil-based printing inks.

THINGS TO DO

1 Photograph 8B shows the china clay working between St Austell in Cornwall and the A30 road to the north.
  (a) With the help of a road atlas draw a map of the area and include the ports of Par and Fowey from which the china clay is sent round the coast or overseas.
  (b) Explain why local people sometimes call these workings the 'Cornish Alps'.
  (c) Find out why china clay occurs on the edge of the granite upland of Bodmin Moor.
  (d) What other industry, apart from the manufacture of paper and board, uses large quantities of china clay?

2 Write out the headings of Table 8.1 and complete it using an example of each of the magazine types described. Write the name of the magazine in the left-hand column and work out the weight of the paper without additives after weighing the magazine.

3 Additives used by the paper and board industry account for about 10% of the weight of the paper. Table 8.2 shows which additives make up the 10%. Choose a suitable method to display the information in the table as a chart.

TABLE 8.2 Additives

Additives used by the paper and board industry, 1988

	(% by weight)
clay	3.2
chalk	2.8
starch	2.4
size	1.0
latex, casein and other binders	0.5
dyes	0.1
Total	10

TABLE 8.1

Magazine	Weight	Approximate weight of additives (%)	Weight of paper without additives
very glossy, e.g. some travel brochures, Country Life		40	
semi-glossy e.g. Sunday newspaper colour supplements		25	
matt e.g. comics, Exchange and Mart		5	

WATER THEN AND WATER NOW

Water is an essential element in the process of making paper and board. Although very large quantities are needed, only a small amount is consumed and not recycled.

Water is needed in two principal ways in a paper mill. Apart from its use in the manufacturing process, water is converted into steam in giant boilers.

The earliest mills needed water to drive waterwheels as well as to dilute the pulp into stock. For this reason mills were built close to rivers and many of them are still producing paper 100 years or more after they were built.

SOURCES OF SUPPLY

Most mills use water pumped from a river or a lake. For example, the Tullis Russell Mill in Scotland uses water taken from Loch Leven. Owners of mills along the North Esk near Edinburgh made certain of their water supply over 100 years ago when they built a reservoir in the Pentland Hills to provide them with a regular supply of clean water.

To obtain pure water and also to add to their other sources of supply, many mill owners have sunk boreholes and pump water up from underground. This is done, for example, at the Tofte Empire paper mill at

Greenhithe in Kent where two boreholes draw naturally purified water from the chalk 24 m below ground level. The boreholes are well away from the River Thames so that salt water brought in by the tide does not seep into the water supply. The water is very pure and can be used directly in the papermaking processes. After simple treatment it is suitable to be used as drinking water at the mill.

9B Water is tested to ensure mills do not cause pollution

9A Water from Loch Leven in Scotland is used for papermaking

WATER USED IN THE PRODUCTION PROCESS

It is essential that the water used in the process is as pure as possible and free of chemicals and matter which will colour the water, such as iron. Only clean, pure water will produce white papers with no blemishes or discolouration. Most mills have water treatment plants that remove unwanted bacteria and dirt from the water pumped from the nearby source.

When it is sufficiently clear and clean it is fed into a **hydrapulper**. This is like a giant mixing bowl. In it the selected pulp is diluted and whirled into a porridge-like substance called **stock** or **stuff**. After further refining and blending with additives the stock is pumped into the papermaking machine.

At this stage the stock contains 99% water and 1% fibre. By the end of the process only about 5-10% of the water content is left in the paper and all the rest of the water is recycled back to the hydrapulper. Improved methods of water conservation have been introduced with the result that the industry's demand for water has fallen. This in turn has resulted in reduced costs. Even so it takes 40 000 litres of water to make one tonne of paper but very little is wasted because of the continuous recycling. Eventually this recycled water is pumped to the treatment plant where it is purified and has any chemicals removed before being discharged into the river. Water Authorities impose strict controls to ensure that discharged water does not cause pollution.

9C Water treatment plants remove chemicals from effluent

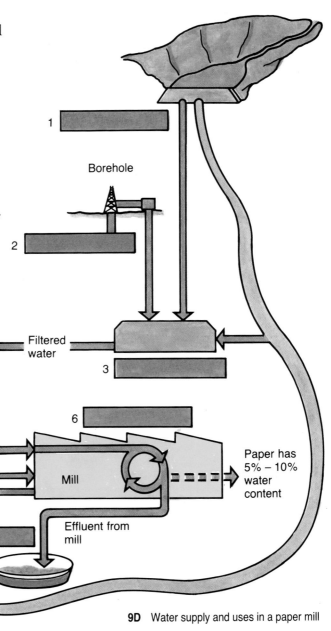

9D Water supply and uses in a paper mill

CONVERSION OF WATER TO STEAM

Most mills operate under a **closed energy system** as diagram 9E shows. This ensures an efficient system with little waste. Giant boilers turn treated water into steam and in the biggest mills this is used to spin huge **turbines** connected to **generators**. These produce electricity in the same way as power stations do. A large mill will produce 60 tonnes of steam per hour. Some of the mills' power houses are so big that they can supply electricity to parts of the National Grid as well as running all the machinery and electrical installations at the mills.

Untreated water from the local supply is used to cool the turbines and then it is returned straight to the source.

From the power plant steam goes to the paper machine where it is used mainly in the steam-heated drying cylinders. The cooled steam is condensed and returned to the boilers as **condensate**. Some steam is lost by evaporation from the dryers. Low energy steam is used for heating purposes at the mill.

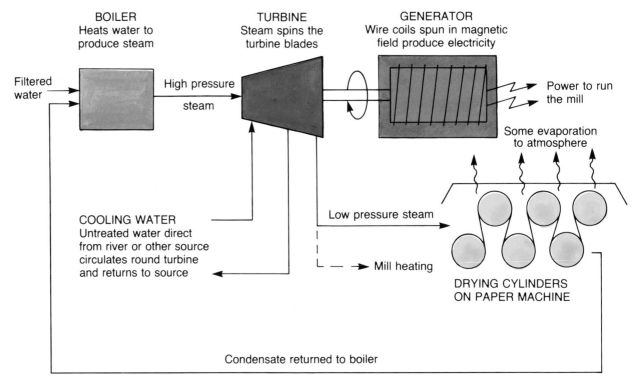

9E Closed energy system in a paper mill

THINGS TO DO

1 Diagram 9D shows the flow of water at a paper mill.
 (a) Write down the correct terms which should appear in the boxes numbered 1 to 7 on the diagram. Here are the terms, in the wrong order.

   processes   filtration tanks   reservoir
   cooling machinery   waste treatment plant
   underground supplies   generating steam

 (b) From how many different sources does the mill obtain its water? Name them.

 (c) Why does the diagram show the water going round and round inside the mill?

 (d) Why does water from the mill have to pass through 7 before it goes back into the river?

2 What are the *three* advantages to a papermill which result from the use of recycled water?

stock has travelled halfway down the wire a high percentage of water has drained away and from there onward the removal of water has to be assisted by suction from underneath the wire.

By the time the thin mat of fibres has reached the end of the wire it has become a sheet of paper, though still very moist and having little strength. It then passes to the **press section**.

This consists of a number of sets of heavy rollers through which the moist paper is conveyed rather in the manner of a huge old-fashioned mangle. The moist paper is carried through this stage on thick felts of synthetic fibre. More moisture is squeezed out of the paper and drawn away by suction.

STAGE 3: THE DRY END

12F Reel up at the end of the machine is computer monitored

12E A dandy roll; the wire shape on the roll makes the watermark

Even at this stage the paper web is still very moist. It then passes to the **drier section** of the paper machine. This consists of a large number of steam-heated drying cylinders, up to 50 or 60 on a fast running paper machine.

Synthetic drier fabrics carry the web of paper round the cylinders until the paper is completely dry.

Partway down the bank of drying cylinders is the **size press**. It is here that a solution of water and starch can be added to the sheet in order to improve the surface for printing purposes.

Beyond the drying cylinders comes the **calender**, which consists of a stack of polished iron rollers mounted one above the other. The function of the calender is to consolidate and polish or glaze the surface of the paper. It is similar in effect to ironing the washing.

Still travelling up to 2000 m/minute, the paper now comes off the machine ready for **reeling up** into large reels, each of which may contain up to 20 tonnes of paper. These large reels are either cut into sheets or slit into smaller reels according to the type of paper and the customer's requirements. The finished reels or sheets of paper are then carefully packed for despatch all over the country or to the docks for export.

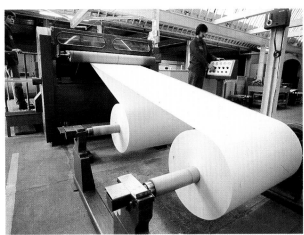

12G Jumbo reels are slit into smaller reels

57

CASE STUDY: AN INTEGRATED MILL

13A Aerial view of Caledonian Mill, Britain's newest mill at Irvine in Scotland. The site is over 1 km long

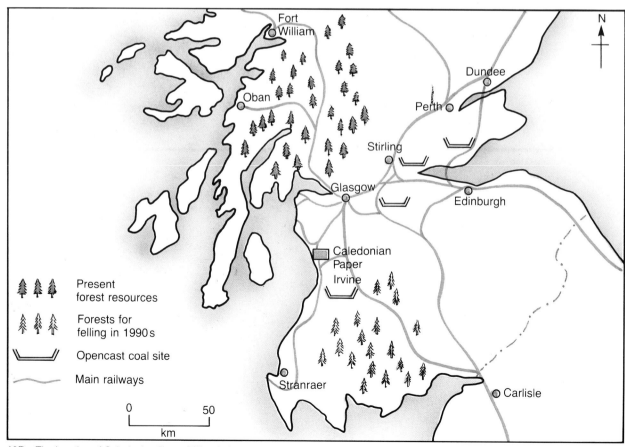

13B The location of Caledonian Paper Mill at Irvine

CASE STUDY: A NON-INTEGRATED MILL

This is a case study of a small, long-established mill producing specialist printing and writing papers.
Company: William Sommerville & Sons Ltd

HISTORY OF THE DALMORE MILL

Paper has been made at the Dalmore Mill on the River Esk (known as the North Esk) to the south of Edinburgh for over 150 years. Production was started in 1837 by William Sommerville, a business partner with John Blackie, the Edinburgh publisher. He bought a mill which had been grinding grain, using the power of the river to turn a waterwheel. Other papermills also developed along the river valley where there was a plentiful supply of water for both power and the manufacturing processes. About a dozen mills were busy making paper in the early 19th century. They used rags from the city of Edinburgh, about 12 kilometres from the Dalmore Mill. Edinburgh was also a market for high-quality paper which was needed by the publishing, printing and stationery businesses. Finance was provided by the city's bankers. Its port was a link with London and other markets, as well

14B　William Sommerville, who founded the mill in 1837

14A　Aerial photo of Dalmore Mill on the River Esk near Edinburgh

as with sources of raw materials. The mill prospered and, after 1872, benefited from a branch railway line. This brought coal and raw materials and took away finished paper. Paper was produced on a Fourdrinier machine and Sommerville's gained a reputation for fine writing papers and paper for the publishing trade. Descendants of the Sommerville family were involved with the mill until 1935 and it still continued as a small independent company until it was purchased by the James River Corporation in 1989.

THE MILL TODAY

All the mills along the River Esk closed between 1965 and 1975, except for Sommerville's which has survived as the last mill on the Esk. One reason why it is still working is the belief of the management that there is a future for a small mill meeting the needs of its customers for 'tailor-made' specialist paper. The range of products includes high-quality writing paper, university degree certificates and paper for best selling illustrated books such as *Queen Victoria's water colours*. About 17% of the output is exported. Over half goes to Europe with smaller amounts to Africa, Australasia and the Middle East.

For many years the mill used esparto grass pulp to produce high-quality papers. Today this raw material has been almost entirely replaced by wood pulp, waste paper and cotton waste. Size, starch and china clay are the other main raw materials, together with

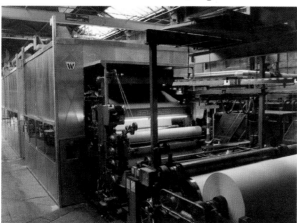

14C The papermaking machine is enclosed to improve efficiency

14D A laminating machine at Sommerville's mill

smaller amounts of dyes and bleaching agents. The boilers are fired by oil or coal and some electricity is taken from the National Grid. The 827 million litres of water used each year are piped from a reservoir in the Pentland Hills. This was built by the Esk papermakers in 1850 to safeguard their water supply. There are about 180 people employed at the mill. Some of these can trace family links with the firm back for several generations. In 1988 production was about 9500 tonnes and included a popular writing paper made from recycled fibres.

The river is not polluted with effluent as it was 100 years ago. Waste water is pumped into a **clarifier**. The solids are removed and the clean water is discharged into the river which is a popular location for fishermen.

THINGS TO DO

1 Find Penicuick on a road map of the Edinburgh region of Scotland. The Dalmore Mill is at Milton Bridge to the north-east of Penicuick.
   (a) What is the number of the main road that runs through Penicuick?
   (b) What Scottish region is this area in?

2 Draw a systems diagram of inputs and outputs for the Dalmore Mill like the one on page 23.

3 (a) Draw divided bar graphs to show the numbers of males and females employed at the mill for selected years. The bar for 1843 has been drawn for you (in bar chart 14E). Use the information in Table 14.1.

TABLE 14.1

Date	Men and boys	Women and girls	Total
1843	25	56	81
1883	86	86	172
1919	46	64	110
1951	90	38	128
1986	133	47	180

(b) Why were more women than men employed in 1843 when rags were used as the main raw material?

(c) Why were more women than men employed in 1919 shortly after the Great War of 1914-1918?

(d) Why are more men than women employed today?

(e) Why do the table headings include boys and girls? Are these headings likely to be suitable for all the dates in the table?

4 Copy the time chart below in Table 14.2 and fill in the right-hand column with important national or international events. The dates of these events should be added to the 'Date' column if they are not already there.

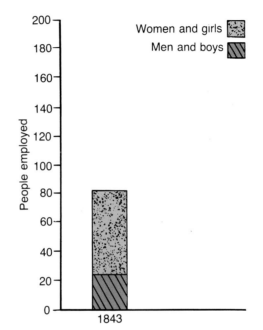

14E Bar chart of number of people employed in mills

TABLE 14.2 William Sommerville and Son Ltd

Event at the Dalmore Mill	Date	National or international event
Started production using rags	1837	Victoria became Queen
North Esk reservoir built	1850	
	1854	Start of Crimean War
Esparto grass first used as raw material	1862	
Penicuick branch railway opened	1872	
Straw used as substitute for esparto	1917	
Esparto supplies resumed	1919	
Esparto shipments stopped, straw used as substitute	1940	
Esparto supplies resumed	1946	
Effluent treatment plant built	1960	
Branch railway line closed	1967	
First computer installed	1979	
'Conservation' recycled paper introduced	1988	

CASE STUDY: A BOARD MILL

This is a case study of a large manufacturer of packaging and plasterboard materials, using waste paper as the raw material.
Company: BPB Paper & Packaging

A VERTICALLY INTEGRATED COMPANY

The company collects its own raw materials, manufactures them into paper and board and then goes on to **convert** them into finished products. The raw material is waste paper and this is collected from ten centres around the country and sent to one of the company's three mills. These are located in Aberdeen, Manchester and Purfleet in Essex. The company also owns a mill in Holland. Some of the waste paper is sold to other paper mills which also use this raw material.

The three British mills together produce over 450 000 tonnes of paper and board each year. This makes them the third largest producer in the UK. Much of the output goes to the company's own converting factories where it is made into packaging items such as

15A Waste paper stocks being unloaded at the mill

■ Waste paper
▲ Mills
● Converters

Aberdeen ▲
Edinburgh
Bangor
Jarrow ■
Thornley ■
Leeds ■
Bolton ■
Radcliffe ▲
Salford ●
Congleton ●
Nottingham ■
Wolverhampton ●
Birmingham ●
Wisbech ●
Aberbeeg ●
Basildon ■
Southend
Perivale ●
London ▲
Purfleet
Southampton ■
Erith ●

0   100
km

15B The BPB Paper & Packaging Group in the UK

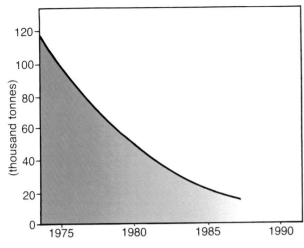

16I Sulphur emissions by Swedish mills

Continual improvements in technology have enabled Swedish mills to reduce the amount of sulphur discharged from mill chimneys by nearly 80% since 1975. As in Britain, the mills are burning less oil and boilers are being designed to work more efficiently. In line with other paper industry companies, MoDo have supported their environmental protection policy with capital investment. At their large Husum mill sulphur emissions into the atmosphere have been cut by two-thirds in the last ten years. In addition, oxygen bleaching methods are being introduced as an alternate to chlorine bleaching.

THINGS TO DO

1 Use the index at the back of a good atlas to find Ornsköldsvik, the headquarters of MoDo in Sweden.
   (a) What is the name of the gulf it is on?
   (b) Approximately how far is it from the Arctic Circle?

2 Look at map 16A.
   (a) How many people are employed by MoDo in countries belonging to the EC?
   (b) Give *two* reasons why pulp mills are located on the coast.
   (c) What problems face ships' captains sailing in the Baltic Sea in winter?

3 Trace the outline of the coast in 16A and mark on your map:
   (a) Ornsköldsvik
   (b) the Baltic Sea
   (c) the North Sea
   (d) the route taken by a ship carrying paper from mills near Ornsköldsvik to Hull.
   How far is the journey by sea?

4 Make a pie chart to show the information in Table 16.1 below.

TABLE 16.1

Where MoDo sells its products	
	%
Sweden	20.8
Great Britain	18.8
France	12.3
W Germany	12.3
Holland	5.7
Rest of Europe	19.7
Rest of the world	10.4

5 (a) What type of ship is shown in the photo below?
   (b) What are the advantages of designing ships in this way?
   (c) What is being loaded into the ship?
   (d) Name *three* countries in the EC to which this cargo may be going.

16J

OVERVIEW

17A Converted paper products

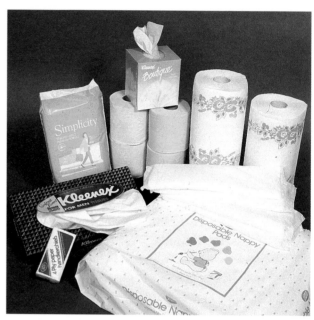

17B Paper converted to hygiene products

A great deal of the paper we use has been processed, after it left the paper mill, by specialist firms called **converters** (diagram 17C). These firms sell their products to the public or to other manufacturers. The manufacture of cartons described in Chapter 18 is an example of the work done by one group of converters. They provide the cartons needed to package the goods of other manufacturers, and design packs to meet a particular need such as the sealed airtight containers in which garden seeds are packed.

Not all paper and board is processed by converters. Some papermakers do their own converting. For example, the manufacturers of soft tissues, such as toilet paper, market their own products and sell directly to the public through shops. They use brand names such as *Kleenex, Dixcel, Babysoft, Scotties* and *Glen*. Some specialist papermakers, for example Wiggins Teape, DRG and Tullis Russell, are also converters. They make such things as stationery products, book covers and adhesive papers.

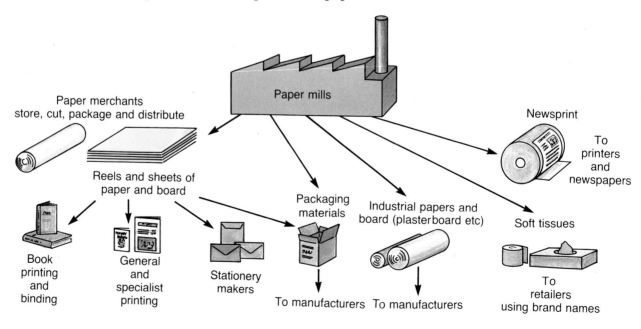

17C How paper and board are converted

PRINTERS

The printing industry converts large quantities of paper and board, much of which reaches the customers as newspapers, magazines or books. The quality of the paper will depend on the product. The higher qualities are used for products designed to have a long life such as hard-backed books. About 65% of the huge amount of newsprint used each day is imported, mainly from Scandinavia and Canada. Three large mills at Shotton in Clywd, Ellesmere Port near Liverpool and Aylesford in Kent produce most of the newsprint made in Britain and distribute it to the newspaper printers. There it is converted into our daily and weekly newspapers.

17E Checking printing plates with colour proofs

In addition to these local printing firms there are specialist printers who have national and sometimes overseas customers. They produce currency and other security papers such as cheque books, certificates and other documents which must be made so that they are difficult to forge. Some large converters also manufacture stationery including envelopes, files, office paper or the lined paper and notebooks which you use at school or for your homework.

17D A printer setting up his machine for printing

In towns throughout the country there are also **jobbing printers** who convert paper and board by printing virtually anything and everything including booklets, menus, tickets, cards, stationery and leaflets for the local market. They are usually supplied with the wide range of papers and board they require by paper merchants. The merchant will help them to select the correct materials in the colours and finishes which will best meet their needs.

17F Printed sheets are collated before being folded

Finally there are converters who make goods of paper and board which we use in the home. Some produce wallpaper using their own designs and patterns for sale through DIY and similar stores.

You might be surprised to learn that the laminates used for kitchen work surfaces are made from paper impregnated with resin. Others make jigsaw puzzles, games or kitchenware such as disposable paper cups, table mats, coasters and plates. Nearly all the paper and board goods we use in the home have been made by converters and new items are constantly being added to the list. Finally, paper is used in the construction of your home — in the plasterboard used on ceilings and walls, on the material laid under the roof tiles or slates and even in the middle of interior doors.

17G A builder installs plasterboard, a converted board material

THINGS TO DO

1 Use the Yellow Pages of your local telephone directory to find the following:
   - newspaper and periodical publishers
   - packaging manufacturers — solid board and corrugated case
   - printers and lithographers.
   (Not all directories will have entries for packaging manufacturers.)

   On an outline street map of your town or district plot the location of these *three* types of customers for paper and board. Use different coloured dots for each type and add a key to your map. Describe and, where possible, explain the patterns made by the dots.

2 What processes will take place to make the following conversions from large sheets of paper or board? Draw a diagram to show the sequence of each of the processes.
   (a) a paper bag printed with the shop's name
   (b) a Christmas card
   (c) a chocolate box

3 The demand for newsprint varies from month to month, mainly because the amount of advertising fluctuates considerably. Draw a line graph from the information shown in Table 17.1 which shows the total number of pages printed in the national daily newspapers during each month in 1986. Because newspapers have pages of different size adjustments have been made to standardise the page size to that of the tabloid newspapers such as *The Sun* and *The Daily Express*.

TABLE 17.1

Month	Total number of pages
January	13 550
February	13 500
March	15 030
April	14 860
May	15 100
June	15 120
July	14 730
August	12 980
September	14 800
October	16 420
November	16 180
December	13 520

Write at appropriate points along your graph explanations of why the number of pages fluctuates.

4 Make a daily count for a month of the number of pages printed by one daily newspaper. Draw a graph to show the results of your survey.

WORLDWIDE CONSUMPTION OF PAPER AND BOARD

There is a close relationship between the standard of living in a country and the *per capita* consumption of paper. We tend to take paper for granted but in the less developed world it is a scarce and expensive luxury. In some countries young children use slates to write on because paper is scarce, just as children did in Britain 80 or more years ago. The paper produced in many less developed countries is often of poor quality and not finished to the standards expected in developed countries. For example, in many parts of China envelopes are not made with glue on the flaps. In hotel rooms, bottles of glue are provided with the envelopes.

In Britain, on average, each person uses 163 kg of paper per year, which makes us eleventh in the world 'league table'. By comparison, the average in the USA is 318 kg. In less developed countries the *per capita* consumption is much lower, falling to 27 kg in Brazil and only 1 kg in Bangladesh. The Developing World desperately needs aid and

20J African schoolchildren sometimes use writing slates

expert assistance in establishing papermaking industries, using local supplies of timber or other plants wherever possible. Some UK companies provide the necessary expertise and advice.

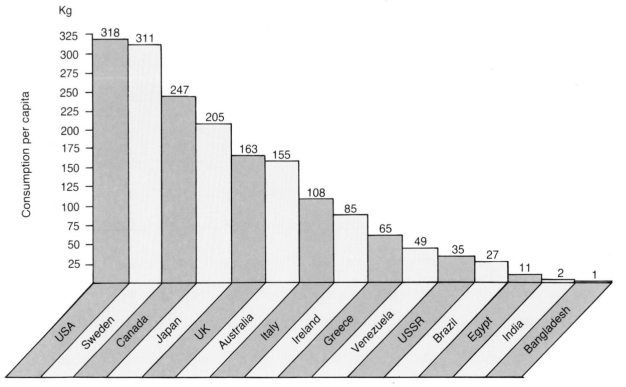

20K Paper consumption *per capita*

THINGS TO DO

1 Draw a pie chart of the exports of paper and board shown in Table 20.2.

2 Are the following statements accurate descriptions of what happened to the consumption of paper and board between 1978 and 1988 as shown in figure 20B?
   (a) Consumption steadily increased.
   (b) In any given year the UK has always consumed more imported than home produced paper and board.
   Describe what the chart shows about the imports of paper and board for the home market between 1978 and 1988.

3 Study table 20.3. Complete the scattergraph opposite to test whether there is a relationship between *per capita* income and *per capita* consumption of paper. A close relationship will result in a pattern of dots sloping diagonally upwards from the zero point. If the dots are scattered at random there is no relationship.

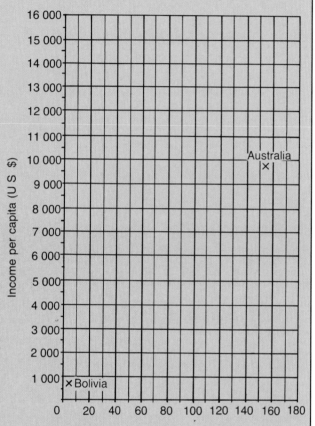

20L The relationship between annual income and annual consumption of paper and board

TABLE 20.3

Country	Income per capita (US$)	Paper consumption per capita (kg)
Australia	9960	155
Bolivia	570	3
Egypt	686	11
France	7179	142
Greece	3260	65
Indonesia	560	5
Ireland (Republic)	4750	85
Italy	6914	108
Japan	10 266	205
Norway	12 432	151
Poland	2750	38
Switzerland	14 408	209
Tunisia	844	12
UK	8210	163
Venezuela	4716	49

CHEMICALS

21I The river Don, near Aberdeen

The paper industry uses a range of chemicals in the pulping and manufacture of paper and board. Those used in the manufacturing process are, for the most part, naturally occurring minerals described in Chapter 8 on Additives. The industry has always taken its environmental responsibilities seriously and during the last ten years has eliminated many dangerous chemicals and by-products from its processes. Mercury and PCBs, for example, were removed voluntarily long before any legislation on their use was passed.

It is important that the industry researches and monitors carefully the materials used in manufacture, especially of products connected with food and personal hygiene. This ensures that harmful substances do not get into food – or people. The de-inking process for recycled paper is often criticised because of the chemicals used and the potential hazard of the effluent. But the effluent is closely controlled and treated before leaving the mill. De-inking is only necessary for higher quality recycled products like newsprint, printing and writing papers when the raw material waste has been printed.

Dealing with effluent is an expensive but vital operation. Many mills have their own treatment plants in order to comply with the strict controls imposed by the National Rivers Authority (NRA) and Her Majesty's Inspectorate of Pollution (HMIP). Water used in the manufacturing processes contains fibres, clay and other chemicals. Unless this effluent is treated and cleaned it can reduce the oxygen in a river to the point where living things can die and unwanted fungi begin to grow.

An example of the measures taken to control effluent is given by the Wiggins Teape Stoneywood Mill on the river Don near Aberdeen. Below the mill the river is used by fishermen. It also flows through a large river park used by the public and then reaches two other mills where the water is required for papermaking. A new plant was installed at Stoneywood Mill at a cost of £0.75 million, in addition to one already in use. Any potential effluent hazard has been removed and the oxygen level in the water has been increased.

21J Effluent treatment plant at Stoneywood Mill, Aberdeen

Over the years 'whiteness' has become associated with clean living, freshness, purity, etc. The advertising industry has recognised this desire for white things and has used it to promote all kinds of goods from 'brilliant white' paint to washing powder and paper. Manufacturing industries in general have responded to this 'white consumer demand' but some of the processes and chemicals necessary to produce white products could be harmful to the environment.

(a) chemical pulp

(b) mechanical pulp

(c) final bleached pulp

21K Three types of pulp

In the paper industry whiteness is achieved by bleaching chemical wood pulp. There are no chemical pulp mills in the UK, but bleached pulp is imported to satisfy the demand for white paper of various types. Bleaching also removes impurities and helps to determine the properties of the paper produced.

Most bleaching involves using chlorine compounds. In the late 1970s Sweden recognised that chlorine bleaching produced complex chlorinated organic compounds which can have an effect on wildlife if discharged untreated. Over the last ten years pulp mills all over the world have been gradually reducing the amount of chlorine used as research discovered alternative methods. For example, peroxide bleaches are now widely used. These are kinder to the environment, as water and hydrogen are the by-products.

One of the unwanted by-products from chlorine bleaching is a group of chemicals called **dioxins**. Although dioxins in pulp mill effluent are being controlled, there is environmental concern that they are present in products made from bleached pulp. Recent advances in analytical techniques have enabled scientists to find minute traces of dioxins in a whole range of substances including paper. The daily human exposure to dioxins has been calculated at 168 picograms (a picogram is a million millionth of a gram). A recent Canadian Government study showed that only 0.7% of the 168 picograms was attributable to consumer products including paper and board. The remaining 99.3% is obtained principally from food, but also through air, soil and water.

The amount of dioxin in paper and board varies from the lowest limit of detection up to about ten parts per trillion. These levels apply for almost all paper products whether bleached, unbleached or recycled. It is very difficult to imagine how small these quantities are so these comparisons may help. 1.0 part per trillion is the same as a pin-head in an area the size of 50 football pitches; or the thickness of a credit card compared to the distance from the Earth to the moon; or the equivalent of 1 second in 32 000 years.

Even at these minute levels there was concern that dioxins could present a health hazard. The UK Government has studied these issues and their report was published in July 1989 (Department of the Environment Pollution Paper No 27). It dismissed claims that dioxins represent a health hazard, particularly mentioning nappies, sanitary and paper products. Pulp bleaching was confirmed as a minute source in the environment. However, increasing levels of

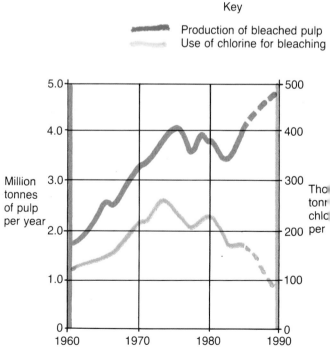

Key

━━━ Production of bleached pulp
━━━ Use of chlorine for bleaching

21L The use of chlorine for bleaching in Scandinavian mills has been reduced by 50% since 1974, despite an increase in production

112

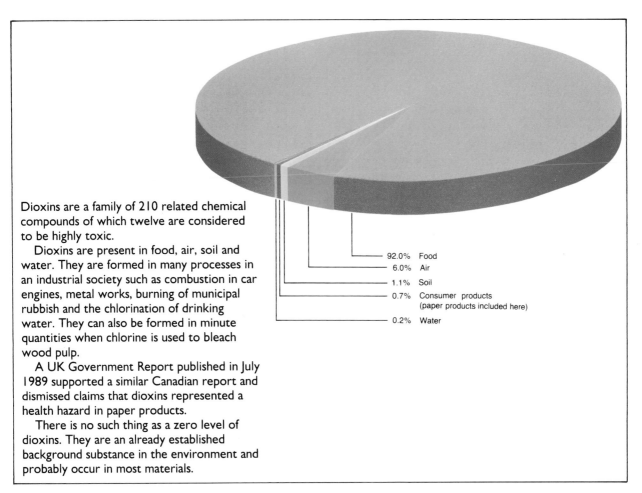

Dioxins are a family of 210 related chemical compounds of which twelve are considered to be highly toxic.

Dioxins are present in food, air, soil and water. They are formed in many processes in an industrial society such as combustion in car engines, metal works, burning of municipal rubbish and the chlorination of drinking water. They can also be formed in minute quantities when chlorine is used to bleach wood pulp.

A UK Government Report published in July 1989 supported a similar Canadian report and dismissed claims that dioxins represented a health hazard in paper products.

There is no such thing as a zero level of dioxins. They are an already established background substance in the environment and probably occur in most materials.

92.0%   Food
6.0%   Air
1.1%   Soil
0.7%   Consumer products
        (paper products included here)
0.2%   Water

21M   Sources of human exposure to dioxins

consumer awareness about the environment are causing the 'green market' to make inroa into the 'white market', and the paper industry is responding to this change by switching to more environmentally friendly manufacturing processes. Considerable choi is available and non chlorine-bleached products are now on the market. It is fair to say that paper only pollutes the environment when it is dropped as litter!

NON-WOOD FIBRES

There has been an increase in the use of non-wood fibres such as straw for paper pulp in recent years and about 9% of the world's paper is made in this way. In some developing countries the use of non-wood fibres could provide a cheap way of making paper using local waste products such as sugar cane, bamboo and cereal straw.

China makes over half of the world's non-wood fibre using mainly rice and wheat straw, and other countries are beginning to follow suit. There are straw pulp mills in Denmark, Spain, Bulgaria and Romania and one may be built in the UK by the British Sugar Corporation. Straw can be used for up to 45% of the pulp needed to make some high quality paper suitable for printing. At present straw stubble is a waste product which is difficult – and sometimes dangerous – to dispose of, as stubble burning, particularly near motorways, has proved. If wood becomes more expensive and supplies less plentiful, it is highly probable that papermakers in the developed countries will also turn to non-wood fibres.

One potential new source of fibre which is being investigated by some North American companies is a plant called **Kenaf** *(Hibiscus cannabinus).* It is a fast growing, non-wood plant which can be grown in rotation with other agricultural crops and harvested annually.

Although requiring large storage areas for the harvested crop, Kenaf mixed with waste paper could provide an economically priced pulp for newsprint production. This combination may well be attractive to developing nations who, by growing Kenaf, would have an **indigenous** raw material and therefore not need to use their limited supplies of currency to buy newsprint from overseas.

Developed nations, while increasing the amount of waste paper they are recycling, have potential supplies well in excess of their own needs. Instead of burying or burning the surplus waste paper it could be shipped to developing countries. This would help to protect the environment and reduce the demand for fibre from existing managed forests.

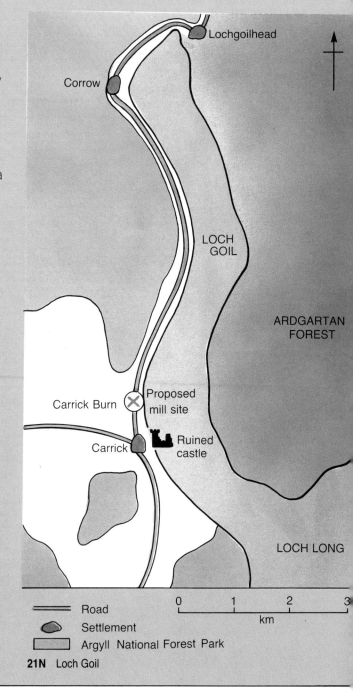

THINGS TO DO

Role play
In this imaginary situation you will have the opportunity to take part in a role play exercise in which different people put their points of view about a proposed paper mill development beside a Scottish loch.

The proposal
The Glenpulp Paper and Board Company are seeking a site for a new integrated paper mill. One site that has been suggested is on Loch Goil about 50 km north-west of Glasgow. The mill would employ about four hundred people and use pulp wood from Scottish forests. The site is close to, but not in the Argyll National Forest Park.

The enquiry
Conduct a planning enquiry in your class with a chairperson and members of the class taking roles listed below. Each person should speak for about two or three minutes and after the chairperson has summed up, the class should vote as to whether the planning application should be approved or rejected.

Points of View
1 A representative of the Ramblers Association: *The proposal would create an eyesore in an area of great beauty.*

2 A representative of the Royal Society for the Protection of Birds: *The noise and pollution would drive away the kingfishers, buzzards and ptarmigan which nest in the National Forest Park.*

3 A representative of the Countryside Commission for Scotland: *A development of this type should not be permitted. It will be visible from many points in the National Forest Park.*

Lochgoilhead
Corrow
LOCH GOIL
ARDGARTAN FOREST
Carrick Burn
Proposed mill site
Carrick
Ruined castle
LOCH LONG

Road
Settlement
Argyll National Forest Park
0   1   2   3
km

21N Loch Goil

Quality control

100 employees
Links being made
with the Quality
Assurance Institute

**Managers and
professionals**

1500 employees
Recruitment mainly
from within industry
Seminars run by
the British Fibreboard
Packaging Association
(BFPA)

**Production
supervisors**

1800 employees
Training programme
organised by
BFPA

Sales

1200 employees
In-company
training

**EMPLOYMENT
IN THE
FIBREBOARD INDUSTRY**

**Transport and
distribution**

600 employees
In-company
training

Maintenance

1500 employees
City and Guilds
HTEC in mechanical
and electrical skills

**Clerical and
administration**

3300 employees
Secretarial and office
skills with BTEC or RSA
qualifications

**Production
operatives**

10000 employees
Training programme
organised by
BFPA

22G   Employment opportunities in the fibreboard industry

THE APPRENTICES

Brian Danbury and Shaun Bennett are **instrument/electrical apprentices** at the Purfleet Board Mills of BPB Paper & Packaging Ltd. They left school at 16, three years ago and are in the third year of their apprenticeship. At St Cedd's Secondary School about four kilometres from the mill they both obtained 'O' or CSE levels in mathematics, physics, electronics, English language and metal work. Shaun also obtained 'O' levels in computer studies and English literature. Their first year with the firm was spent at Thurrock Technical College, on a full-time course in basic engineering skills, training and supporting technical education. At the mill they are assigned to skilled craftsmen to continue their skills training. They also take day release classes at the technical college.

By the end of their apprenticeship, which lasts on average about three and half years, they should have excellent qualifications for their future careers in the industry. They expect to have gained both Ordinary and Higher National Certificates and the Basic and Craftsman certificates of the Engineering Industry Training Board. At the end of their apprenticeship they will have continuing career opportunities to gain Technical Diplomas and Senior Technical Diplomas. They are encouraged by the knowledge that some of the senior management team at the mill started as apprentices and have worked their way up through the career structure.

Brian and Shaun work from 8am until 4pm and have 25 days holiday each year as well as national holidays. In their final year as apprentices they will join the craftsmen on shift work which will give them 11 days off every five weeks. They particularly like the varied nature of their work which does not limit them to one part of the mill or one particular machine.

Recently one summer Brian was sent on a week's paid holiday as a crew member on a yacht sailing from Plymouth to the Channel Islands; he was only sea-sick once! Shaun plays right-back for the World's End football team and cricket for Tilbury while Brian is a keen supporter of West Ham and does some fishing in his spare time.

23A Brian Danbury (left) and Shaun Bennett

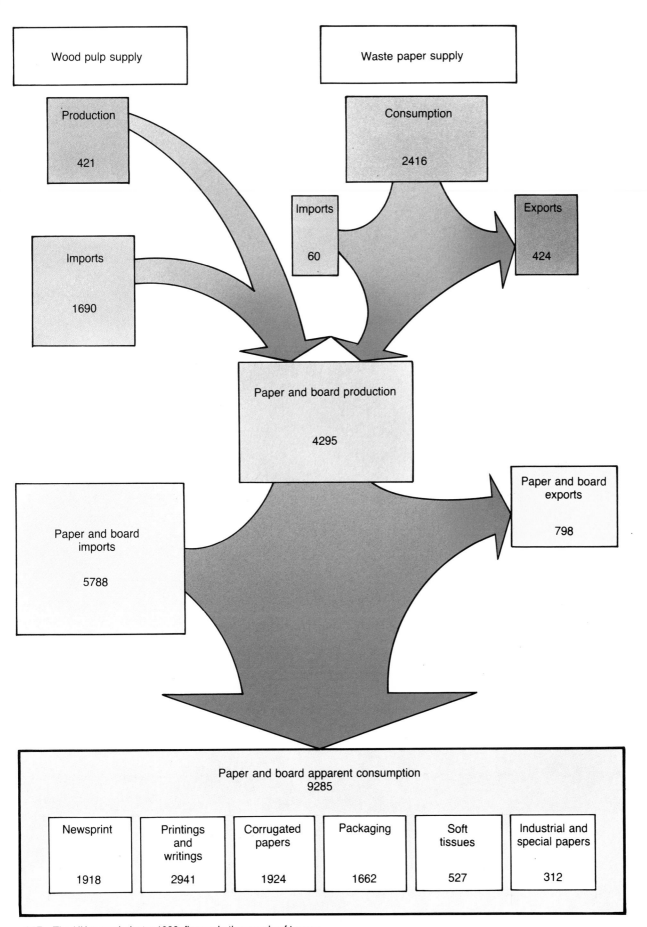

24F The UK paper industry 1988, figures in thousands of tonnes

THE CHALLENGE OF THE 1990s

The removal in 1992 of certain trade restrictions within the 12 countries which form the European Community (EC) will present British papermakers with problems as well as opportunities. Taken as a whole the EC countries are the second largest users of paper and board in the world. They all import paper and board and are faced with competition from the Scandinavian countries and Austria where wood pulp is readily available at low cost. The 1990s may see some important changes in market patterns. The British paper and board industry is, however, in a position to take on competition from within the EC and elsewhere. This results from its capital investment programme and the drive to reduce unit costs.

THINGS TO DO

1 Photograph 24G shows a typical display at a DIY store.

(a) Why is this way of displaying goods becoming more popular?

(b) In what ways are the papermakers involved with displays like this?

(c) List items which could be displayed in cartons or packages like this, but are not at present.

24G DIY goods

2 Make a copy of the chart below and complete the columns to show different ways paper is used in your kitchen. Some examples have been given to help you.

TABLE 24.1

Labels	Liquid cartons	Bags for dried goods	Cartons	Information	Hygiene	Decoration
jam jar	milk	tea	pepper	cookery book	paper towel	doyley

3 In class, discuss new ways in which paper and board may be used in the year 2000.

Here are seven experiments to test some of the qualities of different types of paper.

1 TESTING THE DIRECTION OF THE FIBRES

THE PROBLEM

Paper absorbs moisture in a **humid** (or moist) environment and loses it in a dry environment. It expands when it absorbs moisture and shrinks when it loses it. The expansion and contraction vary according to the direction the fibres are pointing. On the mesh of the papermaking machine most of the fibres position themselves with their lengths parallel with the movement of the wire mesh. This is called the **machine direction**. The opposite direction is called the **cross direction** as shown in diagram 25A. In finished paper the fibres expand about three times as much in their cross direction as along their length. Users of paper often need to know which direction that is. In the mill this property, like others, can be found with instruments. This simple experiment is to find the direction of maximum expansion.

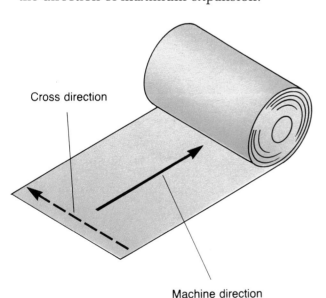

25A Machine direction and cross direction

ITEMS REQUIRED

- one sheet of paper
- a small basin containing water

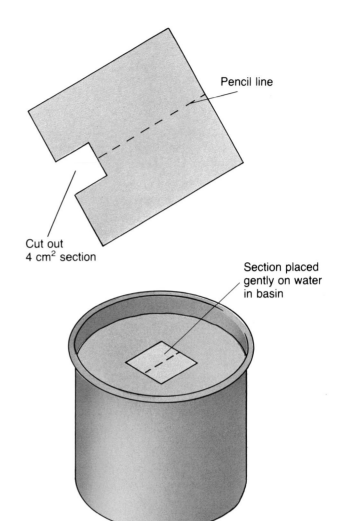

Pencil line

Cut out 4 cm² section

Section placed gently on water in basin

25B Testing the direction

EXPERIMENT

Draw a pencil line parallel to either the side or top of the sheet of paper. Cut a 4 cm square from the sheet so that the line runs through the centre of the square. Place the square carefully on the surface of the water so that the upper side remains dry. Watch how the paper curls in relation to the pencil line. The axis or 'centre' of the curve will always be parallel to the paper's machine direction.

OBSERVATIONS

- What does the experiment tell you about the direction of the fibres in the paper?
- Why does the paper curl?

2 CHECKING PAPER FOR EXPANSION DUE TO MOISTURE

THE PROBLEM

Expansion due to moisture must be minimal for paper to be printed in colours. Colour pictures are made by printing each of four colours separately.

Each colour must **register** with the others. That means that it must be accurately placed to produce a clear picture. If the paper expands while the colours are being printed, the picture may be blurred.

This experiment is to find out whether the paper being tested is suitable for colour printing. Expansion over 2.5% makes it unsuitable.

ITEMS REQUIRED

- a sheet of paper about 30 cm by 21 cm (A4)
- a large bowl or sink filled with water
- blotting paper

EXPERIMENT

Cut two strips of paper, 21 cm by 2 cm, from the sheet, one horizontally and one vertically. Use a fine pencil to make two marks on the strips 20 cm apart. Immerse the strip in water for at least 20 minutes. Take the strips out and place them on a piece of glass or a flat surface. Take off any surplus water with blotting paper and then measure the distances between the two marks.

OBSERVATIONS

The cross-direction strip will expand more. Use this piece to calculate the amount of expansion as a percentage of 20 cm.

$$\text{expansion} = \frac{\text{increase in length}}{\text{original length}} \times 100\%$$

Is the paper suitable for colour printing? Repeat the process with the other types of paper listed in the chart below. Complete the chart and write a short statement describing what the experiment shows.

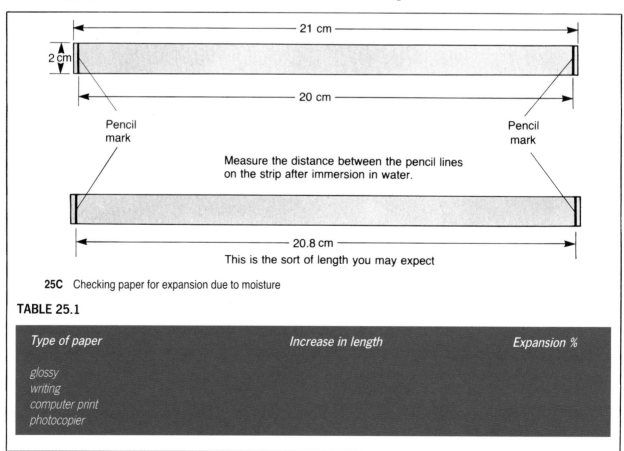

25C Checking paper for expansion due to moisture

TABLE 25.1

Type of paper	Increase in length	Expansion %
glossy		
writing		
computer print		
photocopier		

3 CHECKING FOR WATER ABSORPTION

THE PROBLEM

Unless fibres are treated with size, water is absorbed and the paper is unsuitable for wrapping, writing and fine print work. Absorbent paper is required for blotting paper and newsprint is also absorbent. It is therefore important to know the absorption rate of paper.

ITEMS REQUIRED

- beaker
- coloured water
- paperclips
- three strips of different types of paper
- glass rod

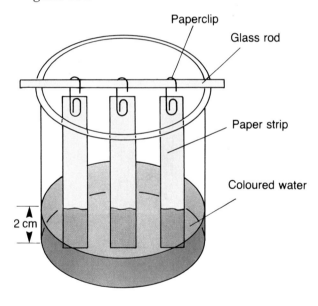

25D Checking for water absorption

EXPERIMENT

Pour the coloured water into the beaker, to a height of 2 cm. Cut the strips of paper the same length so that their ends are in the coloured water when suspended from the glass rod by paperclips. Suspend the strips in the liquid making sure they do not touch. Leave them until the coloured water has reached the top of one strip (probably 20-30

minutes). Note the time it took. Measure the heights reached in the other strips.

$$\text{absorption rate} = \frac{\text{height reached}}{\text{time taken}}$$

OBSERVATIONS

Measure the absorption rates of the other papers and list them in order of decreasing absorbency. Repeat the experiments with other types of paper. What conclusions have you reached?

4 FIBRE IDENTIFICATION TESTS

THE PROBLEM

To identify the type of fibre that has been used to make samples of paper.

ITEMS REQUIRED

- Herzberg stain which is made as follows:

(i)   Mix 5.25 g of potassium iodide in 12.5 cm³ of water.
(ii) Add 0.25 g of iodine.
(iii) Mix with 25 cm³ of saturated zinc chloride solution.
(iv) Stand overnight and then store in a dark bottle. It will keep for about three months.

EXPERIMENT

Put paper fibres to be tested on a microscope slide.
Add one drop of the stain to the fibres.

OBSERVATIONS

Examine the colour change of the treated fibres.
- red − rags or cotton fibres
- yellow − mechanical pulp
- blue-purple − chemical pulp

Repeat the experiment with the paper types listed in Table 6.2 in Question **2** on page 35 'Things to do', Chapter 6. Check your results with the original answers you gave to the question.

5 TESTING PAPER STRENGTH

THE PROBLEM

Design a piece of apparatus which you can
build with available equipment, or equipment
you can make, to test the strength of different
types of paper. Make certain the experiment is
scientifically carried out. Follow these
guidelines and make certain that:

(a) the paper to be tested is held firmly and
cannot move (for example, fix it across the
top of a circular container)

(b) the nail or light weight used is suspended
above the paper and released to fall
without any propulsive force

(c) the dropping distance is gradually
increased and carefully measured until
the paper bursts

(d) different types of paper are measured and
a record kept of the results

(e) an account of the experiment is written
up and any conclusions clearly stated.

6 MAKING RECYCLED PAPER

THE PROBLEM

To make paper at home or school. This
produces a crude material but in carrying out
this experiment you will use similar
techniques to those used by professional
papermakers.

ITEMS REQUIRED

- clean sheets of paper, preferably white,
such as wrapping paper or the non-print
areas of newspapers
- two sheets of blotting paper
- fine wire or nylon mesh (about 20 cm²)
fixed to a wooden frame
- water
- egg beater or liquidiser
- wide bowl (more than 22 cm in diameter)
- a tablespoonful of instant starch
- electric iron

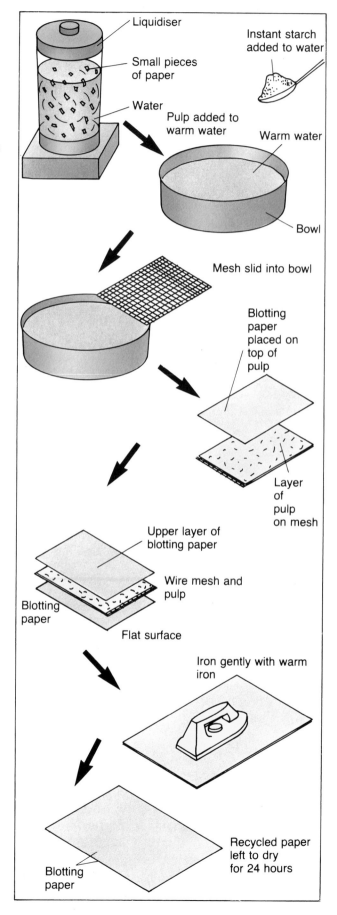

Liquidiser

Instant starch
added to water

Small pieces
of paper

Water

Pulp added to
warm water

Warm water

Bowl

Mesh slid into bowl

Blotting
paper
placed on
top of
pulp

Layer
of
pulp
on mesh

Upper layer of
blotting paper

Wire mesh and
pulp

Blotting
paper

Flat surface

Iron gently with warm
iron

Recycled paper
left to dry
for 24 hours

Blotting
paper

25E Making recycled paper

26F Creative skill and imagination can produce remarkable paper sculptures

(a) Sherlock Holmes   (b) Sir Christopher Wren

COLLAGE AND MOSAIC

These abstract forms of artwork involve creating pictures and designs. Tiny pieces of different coloured papers are used in mosaics. A variety of materials, placed side by side, are used to build up the stunning effect of a collage.

27A Papermaking could be a topic for GCSE coursework

HOW TO ORGANISE COURSEWORK

Companies connected with the paper and board industry are to be found in many parts of Britain although the manufacturing side is mainly centred in four specific areas of the country. Refer to the map on page 25 and to the **Paper Industry Directory for Schools**, which has been sent to your school. This directory lists all the members of the major trade associations in the industry.

There may well be a firm in your district which can provide the stimulus for a project in one of your school subjects such as history, economics, science, art, sociology or geography. Public examinations at 16+ include coursework as part of the examination. An investigation into one aspect of the paper industry would give you an insight into an important British industry. It would also provide an interesting area for you to study and develop as a project.

Having read this book you may already have formed some ideas about aspects of the industry you would like to investigate. Discuss with your teachers a possible title for your coursework topic before planning the investigation. Here are some suggestions to start you thinking.

- The history of a local paper mill
- The science of papermaking
- Cost factors involved in the recycling of paper
- Dealing with pollution at a local mill
- The geography of papermaking in the River Don valley
- Location factors in the siting of a paper mill
- Employees talking about working at the mill
- Paper as an art form
- Converting paper and board
- A local service industry – collecting waste paper
- Papermaking in the past

- Designing book covers
- The chemistry of paper production
- Environmental benefits of recycling paper
- The fibres from which paper can be made
- The role of the paper merchant
- Packaging for food and drink
- The demand and supply of paper in Britain
- World trade in wood pulp
- The development of papermaking machines in the 19th century

Having selected your topic you will need to visit a company in the paper industry, for example a local paper mill or converter, to obtain further information. Refer to the Industry Directory and write to the manager explaining what you are doing and the purpose of your research. There should be no difficulty in getting the help you need provided you show that you have planned your work carefully and know exactly what questions you want to ask.

If a visit is arranged to a mill **remember** that they are busy and noisy places and the more preparation you have done beforehand the better. Write out the questions you would like answered and leave enough space for the answers.

If you want information about papermaking as a whole you should write to the **British Paper and Board Industry Federation** at Papermakers House, Rivenhall Road, Westlea, Swindon, Wilts SN5 7BE.

27B Try to arrange a visit to a local company

27C Children examining a dandy roll at St Cuthbert's paper mill

Not all coursework topics will be based on a visit to a paper mill. You may want to do research by talking to people you know who work, or have worked in the industry. Alternatively you may want to investigate local converters or paper merchants, or the collection of waste paper for recycling in your area. There are many interesting aspects of the industry apart from the papermaking process itself.

There are three basic ways in which you can obtain material for your topic. You can **use your eyes** to investigate local evidence, you can **talk to people** and you can **use documentary evidence**, most of which can be found in libraries. If your study is concerned with the history of a local mill or converter, material may be available from that source. Alternatively, look in the local studies section of your public library and the County Record Office which is to be found in most county towns.

Carry out your research in a scientific manner by drawing up a plan similar to the one in diagram 27D on page 142. This will enable you to tackle the problem systematically and, when you have finished, to present your project in a lively and interesting manner. Figure 27D shows the organisational plan that was made before studying the history of a paper mill. The pattern of research is likely to be different for projects in other subjects, but it is essential to draw up a flowchart like this one before starting the investigation.

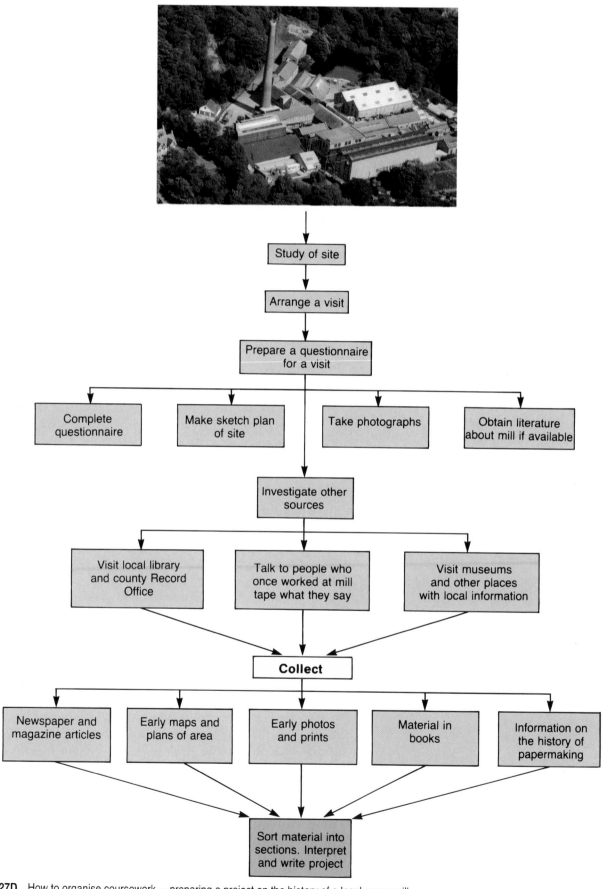

Study of site

Arrange a visit

Prepare a questionnaire for a visit

Complete questionnaire

Make sketch plan of site

Take photographs

Obtain literature about mill if available

Investigate other sources

Visit local library and county Record Office

Talk to people who once worked at mill tape what they say

Visit museums and other places with local information

Collect

Newspaper and magazine articles

Early maps and plans of area

Early photos and prints

Material in books

Information on the history of papermaking

Sort material into sections. Interpret and write project

27D How to organise coursework – preparing a project on the history of a local paper mill

142

CHAPTER 8 (page 43)

1 (b) The tips of waste clay and rock are shaped like mountains and, being white, they appear to have snow on them.

(c) The clay was formed from the decomposition of granite on the edge of Bodmin Moor which is made of granite.

(d) The manufacture of porcelain.

CHAPTER 9 (page 46)

1 (a) 1 – reservoir; 2 – underground supplies; 3 – filtration tanks; 4 – generating steam; 5 – cooling machinery; 6 – processes; 7 – waste treatment plant

(b) Three – reservoir, river, underground supplies.

(c) Process water is continuously recycled and steam for drying is recycled as water.

(d) To remove effluent and clean it.

2 1 – water and steam are not wasted; 2 – valuable materials can be removed from it; 3 – reduced costs to mill

CHAPTER 10 (page 49)

2 The 1988 bar chart shows an increase in total energy consumed of nearly 200 million therms. Less coal, gas and oil were used in 1988 but much more electricity.

CHAPTER 11 (page 54)

Choose site B because it is near the papermills, close to a port and close to a town for its workers. It is also close to good roads to the main town and port.

CHAPTER 13 (page 62)

2 (a) A new town is one which has been built since World War II, 1939-1945.

(b) They were built to help solve overcrowding and poor living conditions in the big cities by rehousing people in new towns quite separate from the parent city. Some have been built to encourage economic development in declining areas.

(c) Cumbernauld, Cwmbran, Bracknell, Telford, Peterlee etc.

3 (b) Help from Irvine Development Corporation; a pleasant countryside and coast; a good workforce nearby; good communications; good leisure facilities

CHAPTER 14 (pages 64-5)

1 (a) 701
(b) Lothian

3 (b) The women were used for sorting the rags.

(c) Over a million men were killed in the war and more trained women were available.

(d) Fewer women train or qualify in the engineering and high tech subjects required in a modern mill.

(e) In the 19th century children were employed in mills until Acts of Parliament stopped child labour. On the chart the headings are only suitable for the 1843 date.

CHAPTER 15 (page 69)

1 Waste paper centres: Jarrow, Thornley, Leeds, Bolton, Salford, Wolverhampton, London, Southampton, Basildon, Southend
Mills: Aberdeen, Radcliffe, Purfleet
Converters: Aberdeen, Edinburgh, Radcliffe, Nottingham, Congleton, Wisbech, Birmingham, Aberbeeg, Perivale, Purfleet, Erith, Bangor

CHAPTER 16 (page 75)

1 (a) Gulf of Bothnia **(b)** 360 km
2 (a) 2647
(b) Ease of export by ship; use of water to transport timber to mills
(c) Icing over, especially north of the Gulf of Bothnia; fog and poor visibility
3 Approximately 2200 km
5 (a) a roll on/roll off (ro-ro) ship
(b) Container vehicles can drive on and off without unloading; turn-round time in ports is shorter; cranes and other lifting equipment at ports is not needed.

(c) large reels of paper

(d) Britain, France, W Germany, Holland, Denmark, Belgium, Italy, Spain

CHAPTER 17 (page 78)

2 (a) paper printed, cut, folded and then glued along base

(b) card printed, cut to size, folded

(c) card printed, cut to size, folded and glued

CHAPTER 18 (pages 87-8)

1 Moisture – non-absorbent paper and waxed cartons e.g. milk cartons

Puncturing – cartons laminated with metal foil e.g. hair shampoo sachets

Damage and breakage – firm cartons, corrugated board e.g. boxes for porcelain

Grease – board laminated with plastics and sized e.g. butter and lard containers

Light – cartons or bags laminated with metal foil e.g. film containers

Germs and infection – separate sterilised wrappings or bags e.g. Elastoplast strip

Sticking together – separate wrappings or cartons e.g. sweets

Crushing or bruising – moulded cartons, corrugated board e.g. cartons for tomatoes

Staleness – sealed laminated bags e.g. peanuts

4 (a) easily packed, cannot break, light to carry

(b) uses self-storage efficiently, leaving no empty spaces

(c) can be printed, coloured and given different shapes

The milkman might find the rectangular cartons difficult to carry.

7 The key words include: carton; fluting; paper; sack; fibre; bag; glue; corrugated; recycle

CHAPTER 19 (page 95)

1 Sales – area sales, estimating, complaints

Marketing – advertising

Buying – stock orders

Technical – quality control, research

Warehousing and distribution – transport

Personnel – recruitment, safety, company pension

Finance – general accounts

Secretarial – office services, computer use

Managing director – take-over bid

2 (a) & **(b)** **Computer terminal** – customer files and stock control

Guillotine – cutting paper and board

Microscope – quality control and paper testing

3 (a) For the tobacco industry

(b) 188 000 tonnes + 94 000 tonnes = 282 000 tonnes.

(c) 33 000 tonnes out of 282 000 tonnes = 11.7%

CHAPTER 20 (page 104)

2 (a) No, consumption was fluctuated.

(b) No, more home produced than imported paper was consumed in 1978 and 1979.

Imports in 1978 were 3.5 million tonnes, which represented 47.9% of the UK consumption. By 1988 imports had increased to 5.8 million tonnes, which represented 62.4% of consumption. In other words, imports gained a larger market share in the UK over the period.

3 There is a close relationship because the dots slope diagonally upwards from zero.

4 Luxembourg

6 January 88 – 45 900 Kr; March 88 – 46 538 Kr
June 88 – 46 155 Kr; September 88 – 46 240 Kr
January 89 – 47 345 Kr; April 89 – 45 985 Kr
July 89 – 44 455 Kr

The exchange rate remained steady during most of 1988 but the pound strengthened against the krona from September, reaching its strongest point at the end of the year. This meant that the pound could be exchanged for an increased number of kronor, so importers were able to get more Swedish goods for their money – imports were cheaper.

From January 1989 the pound weakened progressively against the krona causing British companies to have to pay more for the same amounts of Swedish goods – imports became more expensive.

CHAPTER 22 (page 120)

2 (a) yes
  (b) all three
  (c) engineering career route

3 (a) Wood pulp supplier – 80% of the wood pulp used by British mills is imported
   Paper agent – agents represent overseas mills
   Paper machinery manufacturer – the supply of papermaking machinery is an international business with many UK companies exporting well over half their production
  (b) Wood pulp is mainly imported from the following non-English speaking countries: Sweden, Finland, Portugal, Spain and Norway.

4 two years

CHAPTER 23 (page 125)

1 (a) Employees fell in number by 46.3% between 1980 and 1988.
  (b) Total production fell in 1981 and 1982 and then increased to reach new highs in 1987 and 1988.
  (c) Number of machines has fallen steadily.
  (d) Output per head has more than doubled.
  (e) Productivity of machines has almost doubled.

CHAPTER 24 (page 130)

1 (a) Little space is required to display a wide range of products. The customer can see all the products and select. No (or little) personal attention by sales staff is needed.
  (b) The papermakers supply the cartons and display paper required.
  (c) clothing; sports equipment; vegetables; fruit

INDEX

absorbency of paper 143
acid rain 49, 61,110
additives 40-3, 45, 128, 143
alum 43
apprenticeship 122
Apsley Mill, Hemel Hempstead 51
artstraws 138
automation 21, 50-4

backsellers 124
beating machine 50, 56
Beloit Walmsley 52
binders 42, 143
biodegradability of paper 7, 80, 106, 143
Black-Clawson International 52
bleaching 51, 60, 64, 75, 112-13
blotting paper 42, 143
board 9, 20, 82, 143
board mill, case study 66-9
board packaging 81
board-making machines 52-3
boilers 61, 64
BPB Paper & Packaging 48, 66, 87, 128
breaking bulk 90
Bridgewater Mill, Ellesmere Port 77, 128
British Fibreboard Packaging
    Association 83, 120
British Paper & Board Industry
    Federation 26, 116, 141
British Paper Machinery Makers'
    Association 52
British Wood Pulp Association 33, 119

Caledonian Paper 34, 58-62, 128
calender 56, 57, 143
carbon paper 143
carbonless copy paper 143
careers in paper industry 8, 116-25;
    fibreboard industry 120; overseas
    opportunities 119; paper merchanting
    119-20; sponsored training 118-19
carton board 81
cartons 80, 84-6, 128, 143
cartridge paper 143
case studies, board mill 66-9; integrated
    mill 58-62; international company
    70-5; non-integrated mill 63-5
casein 42
cellulose 16, 19-21, 29-32, 40, 126
Certificate courses in paper technology
    118
chalk 41
chemi-thermo mechanical pulp 32
chemical pulp 30-5, 110, 143, 144
chemicals 40, 111
china clay 40, 42, 59-61, 64
chlorine 16, 60, 75, 112, 113
clarifier 64
closed energy system 46

coal 24, 26, 54, 61, 89
coatings 21, 40-2, 59, 62, 81, 143
collage 139
compactor unit 37
computer control systems 53
computer-aided design (CAD) 84, 86
conifers 108, 109
conservation 72, 74
consistency of paper 53
consumption of paper 7, 26, 103
container board 143
contraries 37, 143
converting 66, 76-86, 92, 143
corrugated packaging 32, 81-4, 87, 143
corrugator machine 82
coursework 140-2
creative work with paper 136-9
cross direction 131, 143
customs duties 97, 98, 101

Dalmore Mill 63-5
dandy roll 17, 22, 57, 143
de-inking 56, 107, 111
declustering 56
degree courses 116, 118-19
demand for paper 17, 18, 27
Dickinson, John 17, 51, 52
digester 30
dioxins 112, 113
direct trading 92
distribution of paper and board 89-99
Donkin, Bryan 16, 17, 51
down cycling 143
drier section 56, 57
dry end 57, 144
dyes 40, 41, 56, 64

Edinburgh 44, 63
effluent treatment 111
electrostatic precipitator 61
employee relationships 119
energy, conversion 47; costs 47; sources
    24, 31, 47-9, 61
energy efficiency 48, 53
engine sizing 43
English China Clay Company 10, 41, 61
environment 7, 75, 79, 106-15
Esk, River 44, 63, 64
esparto grass 28, 64, 144
European Community (EC) 96, 98, 101,
    102, 130
European Free Trade Association
    (EFTA) 96-8
excise duties 98, 101
experiments with paper 131-5
exports 34, 64, 102

feathering 42
Federal Board 128

felt 52
fibre lift 43
fibrillation 56
fillers 40, 41, 144
Firth of Forth 24, 26
flow box 56
fluting 82, 87
folding cartons 12
Forestry Commission 29, 34, 60, 109
Fourdrinier, Henry 17, 51
Fourdrinier, Sealy 17, 51
Fourdrinier machine 51, 64, 144
free trade 101
Frogmore Mill, Hertfordshire 16, 17, 51
future of papermaking 126-9

Gamble, John 51
gelatine 42
grammage 135, 144
greaseproof paper 144
greenfield sites 60
groundwood pulp 30

handmade papers 10, 15, 50, 51, 79, 89
Holder Group 52
hollanders 50, 56
hydrapulper 45, 55
hygiene products 9, 76, 98

Iggesund Paperboard 35, 70, 126
imports 96-103; history 98; significance
    96; sources 96-8; types 98; wood pulp
    33, 107-8, 127
Industrial Revolution 16-18, 24, 27, 50,
    144
integrated mills 20, 33, 34, 70, 82, 144;
    case study 58-62
internal sizing 43
invention of paper 14
investments 94, 98, 128
Irvine, Strathclyde 34, 58-61

Joynson, William 17
'just in time' principle 101

kaolin 40
Kenaf 114
kraft paper 82, 144
Kymmene 59, 60, 128

laminating 10, 20, 64, 78, 81, 144
Lancashire 24, 26, 53, 54
landfill sites 144
latex 42
light-weight coated 59, 62
lignin 18, 31, 144
loadings 40
London Basin 24, 26

machine direction 131, 144
main contractors 52
mechanical papermaking 16
mechanical pulp 20, 30, 31, 110, 144
merchanting 90-3; career opportunities
    119-20
methane 48, 69
mill wide systems 53, 69
minerals 40, 128
MoDo Group 70-5, 124, 125
moisture control 79
monosaccharides 19
multi-wall sacks 81, 87
multiply machine 67, 144

National Association of Paper
    Merchants 93, 124
National Rivers Authority (NRA) 111
newsprint 26, 77, 107, 114, 128, 144;
    cheapness 9, 10; imports 98
New Thames Mill 123
non-integrated mills 33, 107; case study
    63-5
non-wood fibres 113
North Kent 24, 26

opacity of paper 40, 41, 144
origami 137
oxygen bleaching 75

packaging 11-13, 66-7, 79-87, 126, 144;
    board 81-6; paper 81, 87; research into
    new materials 128
paper agents 101-2
Paper Agents Association 101, 102, 119
paper bags 80
paper and board merchants 89-94
paper engineering 136
paper sculpture 138
papermaking machines 24, 50-4, 89;
    location of manufacturers 53-4;
    sections 56-7
papier maché 137
papyrus 14, 87, 144
parchment 14
peroxide bleaches 112
Phipps, Christopher and John 17
pigments 41
plasterboard 66, 67, 78, 144
plies of paper 53
pollution 49, 72, 74, 80, 106, 110
polysaccharides 19
press section 56, 57
primary fibre 36
principals 101
principle of papermaking 19-20, 55
Print, Paper and Packaging Industries
    Research Association (PIRA) 126, 127
printing industry 26, 27, 77

printing papers 41, 42
process controller 123
product manager 124
production areas 24-6
Purfleet Board Mills 48, 67-9, 122

quality controller 123

rags, as raw materials 14-17, 24, 26, 63,
    106; demand for 27-8, 89
rainforests 35, 108
raw materials 10, 19-21, 61; see also
    additives, waste paper, water, wood
    pulp
recycling, waste paper 18, 28, 34, 36-9,
    73, 106-10, 127; water 44, 45
Reed Paper and Board Mill, Aylesford
    77, 128
reeling-up 56, 57, 145
research and development 126-8
rice paper 145
Robert, Nicholas Louis 16, 51
rosin 43

St Regis Paper 34, 128
sales office manager 125
Scandinavia 18, 36, 47, 110
scholarships 118
Scotland 26, 89
secondary fibre 36
security papers 77, 145
sedimentation tanks 74
semi-chemical pulp 32
shift system 116
Shotton Paper 34
sitka spruce 34, 60
size press 43, 56, 57
sizing 15, 42-3, 145
solid board cases 12, 81, 84, 145
Sommerville, William 63-5
specialist merchants 92
sponsorships 118
stamping mills 50, 145
starch 64, 122
steam power 16, 17, 24, 26, 50
stock (stuff) 40, 41, 45, 56, 106, 145
Stone Corporation of America 128
storage facilities 94
storage tanks 55-6
straw, as raw material 18, 19, 113
strong cases 80
supermarkets 11, 38, 79, 81, 85
Sweden 33, 70, 72-4, 96, 112

talc 41
Tate, John 15
technical services representative 123
technical superintendent 123
Thames, River 26, 44

thinning of forests 20, 108
timber supplies 80, 108-10
tissue paper 145
titanium dioxide 41, 42
Tofte Empire Mill 44
training schemes 8, 116-25
transport 24, 54, 70
trees 19, 28, 34-6, 70, 74, 108-10
T'sai Lun 14
Tullis Russell Mill 44, 126
turn-key capability 52

UK Paper 123, 128
uniformity of paper 53
United Paper Mills 128
uses of paper 9-12

vat 52
vatman 51
versatility of paper 10, 21

wallpaper 51, 78
warehousing 90, 91
waste paper 20, 55, 66, 115; demand
    fluctuations 37-8; depots 37; grades
    36, 37; recycling 18, 28, 34, 36-9, 73,
    108-10, 127
water 20, 24, 44-6; conservation 45;
    conversion to steam 46; demand for
    45, 61; purity 45, 74; recycling 44;
    sources of supply 44, 64
water power 1, 15, 24, 44, 50, 63, 89
water up-take 42
watermarks 15, 17, 22, 57, 145
web 20, 50, 52, 57
West Yorkshire 24, 26, 53, 54
wet end 56-7, 145
Whatman, James 16
whiteness of paper 31, 41, 42, 51,
    111-12
wholesalers 90
Wiggins Teape 123, 126
wire section 56
wood pulp 18, 20, 24-35, 55; imports 33,
    107-8, 127; refining 56; screening 56
wood-free paper 32, 145
workforce 21, 61, 67, 72, 116, 124
World War II 18
wove paper 16, 145
writing papers 41, 42, 107

The concept for the Paper Industry Education Project was originated during celebrations of 500 years of British papermaking in 1988. It became clear that the achievements of the past were no more than the foundations for the future – a future to be inherited by the youth of today.

Paper products, the industry and trade are each fascinating topics. The objective of this book is to increase awareness among the younger generation of this intriguing and ubiquitous material and to set out the career opportunities the industry offers.

The idea has been turned into a reality through the unstinting efforts of the authors, editor and creative team, to whom I offer my deep appreciation. However, it is the generous support of the industry that has made it possible. Therefore, special thanks go to the companies and organisations listed below for funding this first edition, which is being circulated to every secondary school, education authority and teaching resource centre in Britain, as free inspection copies.

This support from the industry underlines the importance it attaches to the school curriculum developing an industrial dimension, and its commitment to fostering links between schools and industry at the local level.

Peter Ingram
Chairman, Paper Publications Ltd

In alphabetic order:
J Bibby & Sons plc
BPB Paper & Packaging Ltd
Bridgewater Paper Company Ltd
British Fibreboard Packaging Association*
British Paper & Board Industry Federation
British Paper Company Ltd
British Paper Machinery Makers Association*
British Wood Pulp Association*
Caledonian Paper plc
James Cropper plc
C H Dexter Ltd
Robert Fletcher (Stoneclough) Ltd
G-P Inveresk Corporation
Guard Bridge Paper Company Ltd
Iggesund Paperboard (Workington) Ltd
MoDo Group

National Association of Paper Merchants*
Newton Kyme
Paper Agents Association*
Portals Ltd
Reed Paper & Board (UK) Ltd
Roe Lee Paper Chemicals Ltd
St Regis Paper Company Ltd
Scott Ltd
William Sommerville & Sons Ltd
Thomas Tait & Sons Ltd
Trinity Paper Mills Ltd
Tullis Russell & Company Ltd
UK Paper Group
B S & W Whiteley (1981) Ltd
Wiggins Teape plc

* trade association members have provided
  funding via their association

Students and those employed in education who wish to follow the trends of the paper trade should find the following established periodicals of interest:

Paper (Benn Industrial Publications Ltd, Tonbridge, Kent)
Pulp & Paper International (Miller Freeman Publications, Brussels, Belgium)
Paper Technology (PIRA, Leatherhead, Surrey)
Paper Focus, Paper Market Digest, Board Market Digest (Paper Publications Ltd, Kings Langley, Hertfordshire)